POSITIVE PRINCIPLES

Hidden In Plain Sight

DR. DAVINA SMITH

-Volume I-

POSITIVE PRINCIPLES

HIDDEN IN PLAIN SIGHT

Davina Smith

ISBN (Print Edition): 978-1-66782-002-6

ISBN (eBook Edition): 978-1-66782-003-3

CONTENTS

INTRODUCTION

SOMETHING EXTRAORDINARY HAPPENED during the early days of the 2020 lockdown. As life began to slow down, I began to see things differently. I started finding meaning in things I once considered mundane. The silence was so loud, I began to see and hear meaningful messages hidden all around me in plain sight.

Seeing things differently made me realize that everything and everyone has a story to tell. This book contains timeless principles I have found to be true in my academic experiences, my personal experiences and my professional career in the military, corporate America, and as an entrepreneur.

In each chapter of this book, you'll find a success principle to nourish your mind, body and soul. Allow the principles to reinforce positive thoughts, increase good vibrations, and empower you to learn, grow, and see things in a new way including yourself, your dreams, your purpose, and your potential.

| 1 |

THE GPS PRINCIPLE

LIFE IS A journey that requires constant navigation. A global positioning system (GPS) is a valuable tool that can help you get to your destination faster and with less hassle. Navigation is about knowing your starting point, knowing where you want to go, planning your route, and moving forward to your desired destination.

You Must Know Your Current Location

To get from where you are to where you desire to be, you must be 100% honest about your current location. The first step in using a GPS is to put in your starting point. It is impossible to map a course and know which direction to travel if you do not know your starting point. Are you where you desire to be in life? Do you know where you want to be? It is ok if you are not where you desire to be, personally, professionally, spiritually, physically, or mentally, but if you want to get to your desired destination, you must be 100% honest about where you are starting from.

The Starting Point Will Change

Imagine you are taking a road trip and you drive all day before stopping to rest in the evening. The next morning you continue toward your destination. Your starting point has changed from the previous day, and if you were going in the right direction, you will be closer to your destination.

Your destination has not changed, but your starting point has. If you continue moving and do not remain stationary, your starting point will constantly change. Once you lock in your destination and begin moving, a GPS will constantly recalculate your route based on your current location.

No matter how slow you go, if you are moving forward in the right direction, you will eventually reach your destination because every day your starting point will become a little closer to your destination.

But what happens if you miss your turn? It simply means your starting point has once again changed. The GPS will recalculate based on your new location to get you back on track. Sometimes the GPS will tell you to keep moving forward rather than going back to the place where you got off course.

Sometimes in life, it can be the same way. Making a mistake or a wrong turn does not have to ruin your entire journey. Sometimes a wrong turn is simply the beginning of a new adventure. A wrong turn does not mean you have to start completely over; sometimes you can keep going and still get back on course on the road ahead.

In life, you cannot live in the past. It will be difficult to move forward if you continue to dwell on a bad mistake or a wrong turn that took you off course. Decide to move forward based on where you are right now and every day you can move further from the wrong turn and closer to the destination you desire.

Your current location does not have to hinder how far you can go or where you can end up; it simply defines the best path for you to get from where you are to where you desire to be.

You Must Be Clear on Your Destination

Once you know your current location, you must be clear on where you desire to go. For a GPS to work effectively, you must enter your starting point and your desired destination. If you are not clear on where you desire to go, you may never reach your destination and even if you do, you may not know when you arrive.

Without a clear understanding of where you desire to go, you may find yourself going in circles, passing right by your destiny. You may run out of gas and get frustrated with the journey. You may get tired of seeing the same things repeatedly.

The same is true in life, you must be clear about where you desire to go, or you will never reach your goals or the destination you desire. Without a clear vision of your future, you may let your dream life pass you by.

When you are not clear about the direction you desire to go, you may feel like you are going in circles. You may get tired, lose your energy and drive, and get bored seeing and doing the same things over and over again. It is ok if you are not happy where you are personally, professionally, spiritually, physically, or emotionally but to get from your current starting point to where you desire to be, you must make a decision and be clear about where you desire to go.

Be willing to Change Directions

Have you ever used the WAZE app? The app will guide you based on the best route. Real-time feedback from people who have been there and done that will tell you how to avoid accidents, traffic, construction, and more. In life, you can learn from people who have successfully navigated the road you desire to travel down. However, you must remember that things can change in an instant, and you must stay alert and be willing to change directions as necessary.

Keep Your Options Open

If you think you know everything, it can slow you down on the road to success. Sometimes the WAZE app will take you on an unfamiliar route. The route may be longer in distance; however, based on other factors such as traffic and construction, the longer route may get you there faster. Sometimes in life, it can be the same way. Do not be afraid to consider other options. Things are constantly changing and just because you have always done it one way does not mean it is the most efficient route. There are no shortcuts to success, and sometimes what seems like the shortest route can end up taking longer.

Follow Your Own Path

Imagine you are meeting someone for lunch. They get in their vehicle and plug in the restaurant address. The GPS plans out the route based on their current location. If they were to send you the directions from their GPS and you followed them step by step from your current location, it is very likely you would not arrive at the right destination.

In life, it can be the same way. Do not compare your journey with others. You do not know if you are starting from the same location. You do not know another person's experience, where they are, where they have been, or where they are heading. Do not assume there is only one path to a successful life. You cannot simply follow the crowd, or you risk losing your way, getting lost or ending up on the wrong path.

Do You Know Where You Are?

Do you know where you are? If you don't know where you are, you are lost. If you are lost, have you ever wondered how you ended up in your current location? I remember driving and getting lost. As I drove in circles passing the same location over and over, I said to myself, "I know where I am, but I don't know how I got here!" Have you ever felt that way in life? Sometimes in life, the most important thing is knowing where you are. Being aware of where you are, and acknowledging where you are is often the first step in getting from where you are to where you want to be. While it is important to learn from the past, there is no value in complaining or blaming yourself or others for where you are or your current situation. What is most important is taking the time to slow down and assess where you are. If it is not where you desire to be, then recalculate and start fresh from your current location and then begin moving forward from where you are to where you desire to be.

| 2 |

THE LIGHTS, CAMERA, ACTION PRINCIPLE

Become the Director of Your Life

THERE IS A lot of work that goes on behind the scenes to create a block-buster movie. In the same way, there is a lot that must go on behind the scenes of your life to create a blockbuster life. Directors coined the phrase lights, camera, and action to describe the process of carefully orchestrating and stringing together powerful scenes to create an epic movie.

As the director of your life, you can use the phrase lights camera action to string together positive, powerful scenes to create epic success and a life you love.

Lights

As the director of your life, the first step to living an epic life is to find out, what lights you up? What motivates you? What inspires you? What makes you excited to wake up every morning? When you understand what lights you up, your life will be bright and sunny, and you will be able to see things more clearly.

Light is a source of energy; it helps you see. Without light, there is no sight. Without sight, you may lose your vision. Light can be used to communicate, navigate, learn, and explore the world. Light provides illumination, so you have clarity, insight, and understanding. Light is used all around you and can come from many sources.

Sometimes you may begin to see someone or something in a new light. It could be in a positive or negative way, but it often means you have a new perspective about someone or something. As you grow and expand your mind, your confidence will grow, and you may also begin to see yourself in a positive new light.

When you're faced with a difficult situation, you can find a way to shed light on it. Look at it from new angles, shine a bright light into the dark corners of every situation, and look deep within yourself for a positive bright perspective.

The good news is when you find out what lights you up, you don't have to wait for someone to come and cheer you up and brighten up your life. You can shed a light on any situation and make it brighter. When you do what lights you up, you begin to walk in your natural gifts and talents, and the light will radiate from your life with the power and potential to significantly impact the world around you. By simply doing what lights you up, you not only make your life brighter, but you can be a light in the life of others.

Camera

Once you have established the right lighting, it is time for the camera. The purpose of a camera lens is to focus and direct the incoming light. A lens is used to magnify or correct flaws in a vision. You can think of your mind like a camera lens. You can use your mind to focus the incoming light. Focus on the things that light you up and then magnify the vision of yourself and who you desire to become. Use your mindset to focus on the good things and see yourself bigger, better, stronger, and bolder.

The camera lens is important because it determines the sharpness and clarity of the overall image. Your mindset, like a camera lens is vitally important. It all begins with your mindset, and your mindset will determine what you focus on and the clarity of what you see as possible in your life. You will not see more than your mind will allow you to believe. If you have a small, limited mindset, it is time to refocus and expand your mental lens. It is time for a growth mindset with an expanded focus on positive thoughts, ideas, and big dreams.

Have you ever noticed how much the camera lens impacts the image you see? If the lens is small, cracked or dirty, it will distort the image you see, but if you have a wide lens, it will capture even the images outside of your focus area. You may be focused on one thing, but because you have a wide lens, when you look at the photo, you may notice a butterfly, a bird, a rain-drop, someone unintentionally photo-bombing your photo or any number of interesting things. Your mind can work the same way. Your mind is like a lens, and it determines what you see. When you expand the lens of your mind and develop your mindset, your lens expands, and your vision expands, adding beauty and a new appreciation to the portrait of your life. When you expand your mindset, you are able to see things and discover things you never noticed before!

Action

Action is a process that involves doing something, often with the inten-tion of achieving a target. Nothing happens if you do not take action. If you don't know what to do, begin with taking action doing the things that light you up. Focus on doing what you love, the things you are passionate about, the things that come naturally to you. Then continue to expand the image of your life and believe that anything is possible. Crop out everything that takes away from the picture you want for your life and then take consistent action and go after your dreams.

As the director of your life, you can use the phrase lights, camera, action to write, direct, and dominate the leading role and create a life you love.

| 3 |

THE APPLIANCE PRINCIPLE

HOW MANY ELECTRICAL devices do you have in your home? You may have small devices like phones and computers, medium appliances like blenders and coffee makers, and large appliances like a washing machine, dishwasher, and refrigerator. No matter how big or small, every item you have plugged in is pulling from your energy supply. Being plugged in to too many appliances at once can cause an overload.

Overload Will Cause a Sudden Shut Down

If you have too many electrical devices plugged in at once, everything may suddenly shut off because you have overloaded and burdened the circuit. An overload means to overfill, to put a great burden on, and to put an excessive amount or a great demand on something.

In your home, an overload happens when you have an excessive number of items plugged in, drawing more power than a circuit can safely handle. There is nothing preventing you from plugging in too many devices, so there is a breaker in place to protect you and keep you safe. When the breaker perceives a potential overload, it will shut off the power to avoid damage like overheating, burnout, and fires. But what about you? In life, it is not much different. Do you ever find yourself plugged into too many activities with all your responsibilities competing for more of your time and energy? Do you ever feel overloaded and burdened? Have ever simply shut down after a long day, feeling burned out with nothing left to give? You must learn to say no when too many things are draining your power and energy. You must learn to say no to avoid a potential overload, or you may find yourself burned out and shutting down unexpectedly.

Being Overloaded Leads to a Loss of Energy

An electrician might suggest that two of the common signs of an overloaded circuit is dim lights and lack of sufficient power or energy. In life, it can be the same way. When you become overloaded, your light becomes dim, you don't shine as bright as you used to, and you may not have sufficient energy to get everything done.

Burnout may lead to a loss of energy, and you may lose your drive, your vitality, your dreams, and your spark and passion for life in general.

You Have to Unplug to Restore Power

To restore power and address burnout and overload, you must unplug some things. When an appliance is plugged in, even if it is not in use, it is still pulling energy. Like appliances, you must pull the plug on anything that is draining your energy. Sometimes you will have to pull one plug at a time to find out what is draining your energy, and then you may have to shift some things around to balance and restore your energy.

Electricians describe a tripped breaker as a switch that is not completely on or off. To fix a tripped breaker, you must turn the breaker completely off before turning it back on again to restore the power. Once the switch is turned back on, the power should be restored, but if it is not, you must continue to repeat the process and turn it on and off again until the power is restored.

The same is true in life. You must unplug some things to restore your power. You must unplug everything that is draining you and zapping all your energy. It is time to unplug when you feel like you are not totally on, and your energy level is fading. It is time to unplug when you feel like you are not up or down, but you are just barely hanging in there, lingering somewhere in the middle. Unplugging is the only way to restore your full power. You must flip the switch in your life and do this repeatedly until you have restored your power.

If an electrical circuit keeps tripping, there could be a serious problem often caused by wear and tear, and it may require a professional. In life, it can be the same way. If you keep tripping, if you feel like you never have power and energy, and you feel like you are unable to fix the problem on your own, you may have serious wear and tear, and you may need to seek professional help to resolve the problem.

| 4 |

THE WHEEL
ALIGNMENT PRINCIPLE

Success Requires Alignment

ARE YOU LIVING a life that is in alignment with who you truly are and desire to be? Does what you believe align with the words you speak and the actions you take? Alignment means a correct or appropriate position, agreement, or alliance. Success is about being in alignment with who you are and being aligned with the right people at the right time. It is about living out your core beliefs and living what you believe and believing what you live.

Life is a journey, and your body can be seen as your vehicle, but your mind is like your tires. Everything rides on your mindset, and optimal performance requires a proper alignment in your mind, body, and soul.

An Alignment Optimizes Performance

A wheel alignment is necessary to avoid excessive wear on your tires, and in the same way an alignment in your life will help you avoid unnecessary wear on your mind and body. An accurate wheel alignment optimizes your driving stability and improves the overall handling performance of your vehicle. In the same way an accurate alignment in your life gives you stability and strength as you align your beliefs, goals, activities, behaviors, and other areas of your life.

Alignment is critical if you want to maximize your potential and improve your overall performance; physically, spiritually, personally, and professionally.

Alignment is about creating order in your life by clarifying who you are and who you want to be. It's about sharing your unique gifts and talents with the world and pouring your heart and soul into doing the things you love.

An Alignment Can Change Everything

When a car is out of alignment, the steering wheel may be crooked. The car simply won't drive straight; it constantly pulls to the left or the right. In life, when you are out of alignment, you may also become crooked in your thoughts and behaviors. You may compromise what you believe and make wrong decisions. Misalignment causes dragging and pulling, so even though you may desire to do the right thing, when you are out of alignment, you may be pulled in the wrong direction.

When a car is out of alignment, there may be uneven or rapid wear on the tires. In the same way, when you are out of alignment, you may notice you wear down quickly, and you may feel off balance. You may feel tired, sluggish, and uninspired. But if you have ever taken a car in for an alignment, you understand that an alignment can change everything. The same is true in life. If something is always nagging at you, but you just can't put your finger on it, or if you always feel like there is something more you are here to do, chances are it is time for an alignment. If it seems like no matter what you do, it doesn't seem to work out, chances are you are not in alignment. Success in life requires alignment and balance. When you are aligned with your purpose, positive things will flow naturally into your life, and your life will be exhilarating and exciting.

Causes of Misalignment

There are several things that may cause a vehicle to get out of alignment. Sometimes a sudden impact, hitting something like a pothole, or a curb, going too fast over a speed bump, or getting in an accident can put a vehicle out of alignment.

The same is true in life. Sometimes the road of life can be bumpy. There may be obstacles in the road like a bad relationship, toxic work environment, disaster, sickness, death, or loss, and all these things can throw you off track, and you can find yourself misaligned. Misalignment may cause you to become disconnected from your true self, lose control, become off balance, lose your way, and turn away from your true passions and dreams.

Maintaining a Proper Alignment

To maintain a proper alignment, regular maintenance is necessary. A proper alignment is fundamental to preserving your vehicle and ensuring it performs well. It is not only a struggle to drive a misaligned vehicle, but driving with a bad alignment is unsafe and should be corrected immediately to avoid unnecessary damage.

In life, a misalignment should be corrected immediately. Proper alignment is vital to ensuring you perform optimally in all areas of your life. A misaligned life is one of struggle and can make almost everything require more effort and energy, but when you are in alignment the pulling, dragging, and straining stops giving you more momentum and strength to live your life to the fullest.

When you are in alignment, you will have more energy, confidence, and clarity. You will attract the right people, opportunities, and resources, making your life more enjoyable, meaningful, and pleasurable

| 5 |

THE BIKE PRINCIPLE

Master the Fundamentals of Momentum

HAVE YOU EVER struggled to get momentum to move forward and accomplish something in your life? Momentum is powerful because it creates motion and energy to move things forward.

When riding a bike, you must know the fundamentals if you want to move forward and achieve momentum. You need to know how to pedal, balance, steer, stop, and manage change to avoid potential hazards and risks, because all these things can impact your momentum. The same is true in life, like riding a bike, in life you must master the principles of success to gain enough momentum to continue moving forward.

Leverage is Power

A bike pedal is a lever that provides the leverage to propel the bike into motion. The purpose of a lever is to increase power to be able to lift someone or something to achieve a desired result. Leverage is power; it is the power to influence people, events, and things. Leverage is one way to work smarter not harder.

In life, you can leverage your gifts, talents, abilities, resources, education, and experiences, to influence the world around you. You can also act as a lever and help lift people up, and help others move in the direction of their goals and dreams. Just as a bike uses leverage to move forward with more ease, you can use leverage in your life to move forward and achieve the results you desire more efficiently and effectively.

In life, there are several concepts of leverage; there is financial leverage, leveraging your time, your knowledge and experience, leveraging technology, and leveraging the experiences of others. Leverage is about getting more done and doing it more efficiently, so you can achieve success at a much higher level.

Consider the difference between a toddler bike and a regular bike. A toddler bike does not have pedals; it requires pushing and pulling and exerting a great deal of energy to scoot slowly along. But a traditional bike with pedals uses leverage to go much further and faster. In life, it can be the same way. If you are working hard, expending a lot of energy to move forward but finding yourself only scooting slowly along, you may need to use the power of leverage. Consider leveraging your time, leveraging the knowledge and experience of others, or leveraging technology, so you can work smarter not harder to reach your goals.

Balance is Vital

Riding a bike requires balance. To balance means to distribute something evenly so that it allows someone or something to remain in an upright and steady position. Balance is crucial in life. Without balance, you will fall. You will be unstable and insecure. You must maintain a balance in all areas of your life, personally, professionally, physically, emotionally, and spiritually.

Steer in the Direction You Want to Go

When you are riding a bike, you must steer in the direction you want to go. Steering involves being a motivating force and guiding something that is in motion. Steering is being a pilot and a navigator.

To go in the direction you want to go, you must keep your head up and focus on the direction you are heading, rather than looking down at where you are. Looking down and taking your eyes off the destination ahead will cause you to lose your balance and sometimes you may fall.

In life, it can be the same way. You must keep your head up and stay focused on your goals and dreams and look ahead to where you want to go, or you can lose your balance, and fall.

Steering Requires Motion

Moving the steering wheel on a stationary bike won't move you in the direction you desire to go because steering requires something to be in motion. The same is true in life; to steer your life in the direction of your destiny, you must put things in motion. You can't steer, change directions, or pursue a certain path if you are stagnant and not moving.

If you tried to ride a bike without a steering wheel, it would not be long before the bike would be totally out of control. The same is true in life. Your life can get out of control quickly if you do not steer in the direction you desire to go. You are the pilot and navigator of your life, and it is your responsibility to steer in the direction of your dreams.

It can be easy to get caught up in the thrill and excitement of moving quickly forward, but you must remember that balance is crucial to avoid falling down. While perfect balance in life may not be completely attainable, you must decide what is important and find a reasonable balance between work and play.

Pay Attention to Your Environment

Riding a bike can be exhilarating, but you must pay attention to your environment and be ready to slow down, stop, or change directions to avoid unsafe situations.

In life you must pay attention to your environment. Pay attention to who you are spending time with and what you are spending time watching and listening to. You must be ready to proceed with caution, stop, or change directions if you find yourself in an environment where you are seeing or hearing negative things or being involved in harmful or toxic personal or professional relationships.

| 6 |

THE GARDEN PRINCIPLE

LIFE CAN BE like a garden, and people can be like flowers or weeds. Are you a flower or a weed? Weeds are simply plants that are planted in the wrong place. In life, it can be the same way. Sometimes you can be planted in the wrong place. You might be in the wrong relationship, the wrong career, or the wrong environment. Other times, the wrong people may be planted in your life. Some people are not meant to be planted in your life. It is not that they are bad people, but they can be bad for your life. Like weeds, having the wrong people planted in your life can hinder your growth, reduce productivity, and destroy your harvest.

It's Ok to Stand Out and Be Different

When it comes to weeds, some are easy to spot amid beautiful flowers. You can tell right away they do not belong in the garden. These weeds can be toxic.

In life, it can be the same way. Many times, you will know right away which people do not belong in your life. Sometimes they will be easy to spot, because they don't fit in with your values, beliefs, or character. Like weeds, they do not add value and tend to take away from the beauty of your garden.

Avoid Fakes and Phonies

There are weeds that blend in so well, you think they are flowers. These weeds may even have a few small flower buds to fool you into thinking they are real flowers. These weeds are like fake people who are not authentic. They want you to believe they belong. They want you to believe they are the same as you and have a similar make up. They may pretend they have your best interests in mind and act like they come with good intentions. They may act as if they want to add value and beauty to your life, but they are frauds and phonies.

There are some weeds that will appear out of nowhere and completely wrap themselves around a flower and dominate and strangle the flowers growth. These weeds are like the people who try to keep you wrapped up and trapped in their drama, their negativity, and their problems. They want to inhibit your growth and squeeze the life and beauty from you.

Tend to Your Garden

You are the gardener of your life, and you must tend to your garden on a regular basis. Gardeners suggest the easiest way to maintain a healthy garden is to avoid introducing disease and unhealthy plants into your garden. Be selective about who you allow into the garden of your life. Tend to your garden regularly and take inventory of who and what is taking root in your life. Be selective on who you allow to be planted in your life and be sure to remove harmful weeds immediately.

Inspect the Root

You must learn how to recognize a weed from a flower and a healthy plant from a sick plant. In the same way, you must learn how to recognize a healthy relationship from one that is depleting you and making you sick.

You must assess the quality of what comes in and out of your garden. Gardeners suggest not simply looking at the top of a plant but inspecting the root quality.

In the same way, do not judge a person based on the outside. People can look good and sound good, but take time to inspect the root, their foundational beliefs and character, their behaviors and integrity. Ask yourself if their words align with their actions? Do they follow through on their promises? Are they bringing beauty to your life or are they stifling your growth and progress?

You are the gardener of your life, and you must take time to clean out the weeds. Surround yourself with people who cause you to grow, people who are authentic and people who add beauty to your life.

| 7 |

THE LABOR PRINCIPLE

LABOR IS THE precursor to giving birth. Labor is necessary for physical birth and for giving birth to your dreams, goals, and visions.

When you become pregnant, it takes a lot of growing on the inside to start showing on the outside. Although you may feel the changes taking place immediately on the inside, you may not immediately see the changes on the outside.

The same is true in life. Personal growth begins on the inside. You will feel the changes on the inside in your mindset, in your heart, and in your soul. You will feel yourself growing and changing on the inside before you see the changes on the outside. It may take a lot of growing on the inside before others can see the growth manifesting on the outside. You must understand that giving birth to the new you, the best version of you that is growing on the inside, will require going through the process of labor, and it may require hard work, great effort, toil, travail, and grind.

As a mother, one thing I know is you will not give birth without some pain, and it is a process. No birth is the same. Each birth can be harder, faster, slower, or easier, and each birth comes with its own set of challenges.

In life, it is the same way. To give birth to your dreams and goals, you must go through the process, and you will likely endure some pain. You may have to push harder than you have ever pushed in your life. It may not happen as fast or as easy as you would like, and unfortunately, things don't always work out the way you planned. You may not always give birth on the day you expect it. You may even experience false labor along the way. Sometimes dreams even die.

In life, you may not always hit your goal the first time or on target, and you may not give birth to your dreams when you want to, but you must not give up. It may take longer than you planned. There may be bad news along the way, threatening the outcome or delivery, but the best thing you can do is stay prepared and be ready to give birth at any moment. The truth is your dreams and your goals just like a baby must be birthed. Whether you give birth early, late, or right on time, the dream inside of you must be birthed; they cannot live on the inside of you forever.

Life is full of uncertainty and let downs. There are times when you do all of the hard work and come home empty-handed because things did not work out as you planned. Some dreams die, but you still must complete the process. It is ok to grieve; it is ok to cry, but then you must learn to dream again. Plant new seeds or try a different approach, but you must see the process through and make your dreams a reality that you can see, touch, and love.

Prepare for Labor

Labor can be difficult, and it requires preparation. If you want to birth the dreams inside of you, you must first prepare! Prepare your mind and prepare your body. Labor is hard work, and you will need to be mentally and physically prepared to go the long haul. You can prepare your mind with positive books, surround yourself with positive people, and enlist support from those who have experience and proven success. Prepare your body with rest, exercise, and a healthy diet.

Develop Your Plan

You must develop your plan. Know the 5 W's—"Who what, why, when, and where"—of your plan. Your overall goal should not change, but you should remain flexible in your approach. Life is always subject to change. It is ok to change the plan but stay focused on your overall goals.

Push Through the Pain

Understand there will be pain. It will be difficult, and it will hurt, but commit to seeing the process through. You must push through the pain. Don't give up! Everyone's experience is different; do not get discouraged if someone else's experience looks easier, or faster. You must go through your own process, and you must push through the pain if you want to see the results of your labor.

| 8 |

THE KITE PRINCIPLE

THERE IS SOMETHING liberating about watching a kite take flight and sway and dance through a blissful blue sky. Do you ever dream of experiencing a similar sense of freedom? The freedom of taking off and going to higher levels personally and professionally. A feeling of peace and contentment as you soar through life, so carefree that nothing can keep you down.

The Winds of Life

When it comes to flying a kite, the perfect condition is when the winds are blowing. The wind is not a hindrance, but rather the wind is a necessary component to help pick the kite up, so it can float through the air.

The same can be true in life. Sometimes the winds of life are not blowing to hinder you; they are blowing to create the right conditions to help you get off the ground and take flight. Sometimes the winds of life are blowing to nudge you, so you will get up and get moving. You don't have to let the difficult situations of life knock the wind out of you. Instead, you can allow the wind to become a source of power that lifts you and helps you soar higher. You can ride the winds of change and accomplish anything you desire. Let go of your fears, negative thoughts, and limiting beliefs and embrace the winds of change, so you can soar in the direction of your dreams!

Get off the Ground

Have you ever felt like you just couldn't get started? Like you needed a little help getting off the ground? One of the biggest challenges when flying a kite is simply getting it off the ground. Sometimes in life, it can be the same way. Then once a kite finally gets off the ground, it may spiral out of control and end up right back where it started. In life, it can be the same way. Getting off the ground can require facing your fears and taking the first step into something new, or something unknown, but sometimes like a kite, when you finally make a little progress, you may feel like you are spiraling out of control ending up right back where you started. Do not give up! Get back up and try again.

Don't Let People Pull Your Strings

When a kite begins to nosedive, the natural reaction is to pull the string tighter to keep it from falling. The problem is, the short line gives too much control to the person holding the string and limits the kites freedom and ability to fly. In life, it can be the same way; sometimes you can give other people too much control over your life, and it can limit your freedom and ability to soar. Do not allow people to put you on a short string with their limiting mindsets and small dreams. Do not allow people to put limitations on your dreams, your goals, your beliefs, and your expectations. Don't allow people to pull your strings so tight, it causes you to spiral out of control or hinders your ability to move through life freely. You must separate yourself from anyone who hinders you from getting off the ground and interferes with your ability to soar. Make sure you are the one holding the strings, so you can take the limits off, loosen the reigns, and give yourself the freedom to fly.

There Are Always Strings Attached

The string on a kite may seem like a hindrance, but it is designed to provide safety, stability, and direction. A kite cannot fly safely without the string. It will become out of control before it comes crashing down and is destroyed and damaged. The same is true in life. Your mindset is like the string on a kite. A negative mindset is like a kite without a string. It may lack control and is prone to crashing and destruction. But a positive powerful mindset is like a string that will keep you stable and move you in the right direction. Maintaining a positive mindset will lift your mood and help you become more optimistic. As you begin to transform your mindset to one of positivity and faith, you will be able to soar like a kite and rise high above the challenges of life.

However, even with a positive mindset, life will not be perfect. There will be seasons where you are up and seasons when you are down. There are seasons where it feels like you simply can't get off the ground. There may be times when you feel like nothing is moving, and there may be other times when you feel like you are soaring through life. There will be times when the winds of life take you to higher heights and other times when the winds will blow so violently, they threaten to take you off course. But remember, like a kite, you are made to fly! Make the most of every season and every opportunity in life, and ride the winds of change to the destiny you desire.

| 9 |

THE RECIPE PRINCIPLE

IMAGINE THE PERFECT recipe. Your mouth may begin to water at the mere thought of enjoying your favorite treat. But what about the perfect recipe for success? A good recipe will tell you the essential ingredients you need, how to mix them together, the time involved, and what you can expect from the final product. Once you choose a recipe, all you have to do is follow it step by step to achieve the desired outcome.

Finding the Right Recipe

Life is not as simple as finding a recipe and recreating it. You may not be able to find a recipe that has all the ingredients you enjoy. In your career, you may not find a job that has everything you are looking for. When searching for a home, you may not find the perfect home with all the amenities you desire. Other times you may find you are missing some of the ingredients you need to create the life you desire. You may not have the resources, education, or faith to create the recipe you desire. However, there is not one single recipe for success. If you have ever searched google for a recipe, you probably found hundreds of recipes for the same dish. In life, it is the same way. If you do not find the perfect job, you can create your own business. If you don't find the perfect house, you can have one custom built and you can create your own recipe for success. You can add your uniqueness and use your gifts and talents as the secret ingredients for cooking up a successful life you will love.

Follow a Proven Recipe

You can figure it out on your own, but be open to learning from others to avoid doing things the hard way. Sometimes trying to figure it out on your own can hold you back and slow down your progress. You should remember there is nothing wrong with seeking advice from people you respect and trust. Life is short and you don't have to make all the mistakes yourself. You can speed up and improve your progress when you are willing to learn from the mistakes of others.

Decide What You Want

Over the last few years, companies have begun shipping boxes with fresh food ingredients and step by step recipes right to your home. It is virtually impossible to mess up the recipes if you have patience, follow the instructions, and pay attention to details.

These step-by-step recipes in a box remind me of our everyday lives. First you must decide what you want. You must pick which recipes you want to create. Just as in real life, it all begins with deciding what you want to create and what you want your life to look like.

Take Inventory

When the box arrives, you must take inventory, and make sure you have all the items you need to complete the recipe.

An inventory is a complete list of your most important assets. In life, you must consider your assets and determine what else you might need to add to your inventory to create the life recipe you desire.

Do the Work

Finally, you must do the work. You must take the time to follow the instructions. If you want the same exact results, do not take shortcuts, or make substitutions. There is absolutely nothing wrong with altering a recipe to fit your specific needs, but you must understand that any alterations will cause you to get a different outcome. In life, you cannot expect to substitute laziness for hard work and get the same results as someone who works hard.

Quality Ingredients Matters

If you put low quality ingredients in a recipe, you will end up with a low-quality recipe. Whatever you put in is what you will get back out. In life, your experiences, your mindset, your skills, your passion, and your drive are the most important ingredients to creating a successful life. Like cooking, whatever you put in is what you will get back out, so you must constantly grow and improve yourself.

You Must Have the Right Tools

Having the right resources can make things easier and speed up your progress. Manually mixing a recipe that calls for an electric mixer will require extra time and energy, and your results may not be as smooth. In the same way, if you do not have the right resources and tools in life, it can hinder your personal and professional progress. It is still possible to get the job done, but it may take you longer, and you may not get the best results without the right tools.

Rate Your Recipe

After every meal, rate your recipe. Determine what went well, what could be done better, and what you will do differently next time? The first time you make a recipe, you may follow it exactly, but the next time, you might put your own spin on it and make it more personal. After you enjoy your recipe, share it with others. The same is true in life. Everyday ask yourself, what went well, what could I do better, and what will I do differently next time? As you make improvements and put your own spin on things, do not be afraid to share your new recipes for success with others.

Be Patient, Be Creative, and Experiment

You may not be a perfect chef the first time you attempt a recipe. You may get your hands dirty, and it can get messy. Cooking requires patience, experimentation, and creativity. With time, you will learn when and how to apply substitutions that will enhance your recipes and make them personal.

The same is true in life. Success requires you to get your hands dirty and put in the work. Sometimes it can look messy during the process. Success requires patience, experimentation, and creativity. Seek progress, not perfection. In life, you learn by doing. Experience is often the best teacher, and your experiences will allow you to create your own success recipes. With time, you will learn how to duplicate your success and substitute items to enhance your success and live a life you love.

| 10 |

THE WATER PIPE PRINCIPLE

WATER PIPES ARE designed to allow things to flow and move with ease and little effort, but when a problem exists, the flow is often interrupted.

A flow is a steady continuous stream, but flow has also been described as complete concentration. There are often subtle signs that a pipe is on the verge of busting. You may experience low water pressure or a sporadic flow.

In life there may be times when you notice a disruption in your flow. You may feel distracted. Things may not be running smoothly, and everything may seem to require more effort. You may move sluggishly, or you may find yourself starting and then stopping because you are physically, mentally, or emotionally exhausted. These may be signs that you are getting to a breaking point, and you might suddenly start to fall apart and break.

Too Much Pressure

One reason a pipe may burst is water pressure. Intense water flow can cause the pipes to expand to the point of breaking.

In the same way, when the pressure is too great, in your life, you may get to the point where you feel like you will break and explode.

Storms of Life

Sometimes a pipe might burst because of the weather. When ice builds up in the pipes it causes pressure to build up and the pipe may rupture under the pressure.

In life, when you go through cold, icy, difficult seasons, you may become frozen and frustrated, and the pressure can build up to the point where you explode under the pressure.

Obstructions and Difficulties

Clogging is another reason pipes may bust. Sometimes things can become clogged or stuck in the pipes, causing the pipes to burst.

Sometimes in life, you may go through situations where you feel like your path to success is obstructed or you are stuck. You may feel like your progress is being hindered or obstructed by difficulties and challenges.

Exposure

Sometimes pipes may be exposed and not properly protected. When pipes are exposed to the elements or subjected to above-ground mistreatment, they gradually become damaged to the point that they crack and break.

In the same way, when you are subjected to mistreatment or exposed to negative people and situations, you may become damaged to the point that you crack and break.

Cracked Pipes

Cracked pipes often burst, so it is vital to conduct regular inspections to prevent damage. You may face situations in life that cause you to feel cracked and broken. You must constantly take inventory and do a close inspection of your life to search for areas of brokenness, hurt, anger, and unforgiveness that could lead to an explosion.

Identifying and Fixing Problems

Ideally, it would be great to identify the problems and fix them before they get out of hand, but what do you do once a pipe bursts? How do you avoid the most damage?

Shut it Down

First, shut it down. Bring the water to a stop to prevent further damage. In life, you need to shut down the nonsense, the drama, the stress, the negative thoughts, and whatever is causing you harm. Shut it down immediately to prevent further damage.

Locate the Problem

To fix a pipe, you must locate the broken pipe and then inspect the damage. You can only ignore the problem for so long, but once the problem rears its ugly head, it must be addressed.

In life, there comes a time when you must examine your life and inspect the damage, the hurt, and the loss. To address your problems, you must know what is broken and what needs to be repaired. Once you identify the problem, it is time to conduct the repairs. Pull out the tools and prepare to get dirty. Prepare for the possibility that it might get messier before it gets fixed.

When it comes to repairing areas in your life that need healing, mending, or restoring, it may require many resources and tools, and it may get a little messy before it is fixed. The truth is, sometimes it may require calling in a professional or someone with more experience.

For a water problem, you might call a restoration company, but for a life problem, you might call in a restoration counselor, a friend, a co-worker, or anyone you love and trust to help you restore your breaks and hurts.

Warning Signs

You must learn the warning signs, conduct regular maintenance, and know how to address the problem to prevent further damage.

It is important to understand that it is ok to call for help if it becomes too much for you to handle on your own. Take an assessment of your life today, pay attention to the early warning signs, and make a point to address any areas that might need attention.

| 11 |

THE ROLLER SKATE PRINCIPLE

SKATING MAY NOT come naturally to everyone, and if you do not skate on a regular basis, you may get a little rusty. Skating takes patience and practice and even an expert is at risk of falling.

If You Fall, Pick Yourself Up

Every skater may fall at some point, but its ok, simply pick yourself up and keep going. In life, it is the same way. There are times when you may fall, and it is ok; it's a part of the learning experience. Simply get back up and keep going.

The key to success is to always get back up and keep going. You may have to take it slow until you get the hang of it, and that is ok too. It does not matter how slow you are going as long as you continually move and make progress in the right direction.

On the skating rink, sometimes, the slower skaters will disrupt the flow of the more experienced skaters. In life, it can be the same way. Don't allow people to come into your life and disrupt your flow when you are on a mission. No matter what keep moving.

Like many activities, you can't learn to skate by reading about it; you learn by putting on the skates and getting on the rink. The same is true in life, you will learn by doing, by getting your wheels turning in life, and moving in the direction of your dreams.

Don't Compare Yourself to Others

There is always going to be someone better than you, so don't waste your time comparing yourself to others. You never know how much experience someone else has. You do not know how long or how often other people practiced to become proficient in their skill, so it makes no sense to compare yourself to them. Rather than comparing yourself to others, learn to observe others and learn from them. You might even seek out others who have skills that you desire to learn. Ask questions, listen, and be coachable. There will always be someone who is better than you, smarter that you, has a better position, more education, or appears to be moving through life faster and smoother than you, but comparing yourself is a miserable way to live. You should only compare yourself to the person you were yesterday and the person you want to become tomorrow. Set your own goals, and then measure your success by your personal growth and your ability to reach your personal goals.

Forget about Looking Silly

Forget about who is watching, and don't worry about looking silly; have fun, live in the moment, and just enjoy each and every experience.

Have you ever experienced that unique sense of freedom on the skating rink where all you hear is the music? It is as if the crowds fade, and you don't have a care in the world. You forget about falling or looking silly. You forget about how you look, and you simply enjoy the moment. You are no longer concerned about who is watching you or judging you; you are simply enjoying the experience.

In life, sometimes it can take longer to get to that same level of independence. Sometimes you may be too concerned about looking silly. You might wonder, what will people say if I start that business? What will people say if I start this new sport or hobby at my age? What will people say if I am the oldest one in the graduating class? But you should learn to forget about what people are saying, forget about looking silly; follow your heart, enjoy the experience, have fun, get over your fears, and dominate your life.

Live life and take some risks. Taking a risk means there is a chance that things will not work out the way you plan. You may fall, but if you do, get back up! Be the best that you can be! Don't compare yourself to others and stop worrying about what other people think or say. Live your life unapologetically. Dominate your life, overcome your fears, and enjoy your life to the fullest.

| 12 |

THE BALLOON PRINCIPLE

HAVE YOU EVER noticed the power balloons have to illuminate a room and make it bright and cheerful? Balloons are used for parties, celebrations, festivities, and a variety of significant events throughout life. Despite their simplicity, balloons can take any event from ordinary to extraordinary.

Have you ever wished you could be the kind of person who makes a room bright and cheerful and is always rising to the top? Whether you are an introvert or an extravert, it is possible to be bright and cheerful and rise to the top in every situation. The key is to pay attention to what you allow to fill your life. A balloon will rise higher or sink to the ground, based on what it is filled with. The same is true in life. Whatever you put in your mind determines whether you will rise to the top or whether you will sink to the bottom.

Whatever you consume, the things you read, listen to, watch, the things you believe, and the people you surround yourself with, will fill you up and dictate your mood, your beliefs, and the direction you go in life.

If you choose to fill your life with negative and harmful thoughts and people, it will keep you down. You will be negative and gloomy. But if you fill your life with positive, enriching material and supportive and encouraging people, it will elevate you, inspire you, lift you up, empower you, motivate you, and cause you to be bright and cheerful and brighten up the world around you.

Don't Walk Around Deflated

Without the right balance, a balloon cannot fulfill its purpose. A balloon with too much pressure will burst, and a balloon with too little air will be deflated. Deflated means to reduce in size or effectiveness or cause to contract or shrink.

In life, it is the same way. You can't fulfill your purpose if you are walking around deflated. There will be times in your life when the demands, expectations, and daily challenges can leave you feeling emotionally and physically deflated, but don't allow the challenges of life to shrink the size of your dreams or diminish your zeal for life. Just as a balloon must be filled up and expanded to fulfill its purpose, you must fill your mind with positive expanding thoughts. You must fill your mind with faith, hope, love, positivity, powerful experiences, and positive ideas and thoughts so you can grow, expand, and accomplish your purpose.

If you truly want to accomplish the purpose you were designed for, you cannot walk around empty and deflated. You must be purposeful and deliberate about growing. Preparing a balloon requires a little stretching before filling it with fresh air. The same is true in life, be willing to stretch yourself and fill your life with a breath of fresh air, with new experiences, ideas, and opportunities that support your dreams and help you to grow and reach heights higher than you have ever imagined.

Too Much Pressure Is Dangerous

Balloons are made to handle pressure, but they have a limit, and too much pressure will cause them to burst. The same is true in life.

You are resilient, and you are made to handle stress and pressure, but if you allow too much pressure to build up on the inside of you, you could burst. You must find ways to handle the pressure of your stressors. You must find what helps you to decompress. Maybe its exercise, going for a walk, spending time in nature, listening to music, spending time with family, or reading a book, but you must find ways to release the pressure before you explode.

Sometimes You Have to Let Go

Have you ever blown-up balloons to decorate for a party or event? After the event, it may have been hard to let the balloons go because for a time they brought so much joy, and you put so much of your own breath, time, and energy into them.

Sometimes you may invest your time and energy into a relationship, a company, or a career, and it can be hard to let it go because you have put your time and energy into them. But there is a time and a season for everything, and sometimes you must let things go.

Letting go is never easy, but if you have ever let go of a balloon filled with helium, you know that when you let it go, it will float away and get smaller and smaller, eventually disappearing into a little speck in the sky. The next time you find yourself facing a challenge, imagine you are holding a balloon or several balloons tightly in your arms. Each balloon represents your challenges and all the things that stress you out and keep you up at night. The balloons represent all the things that worry you, your hurts, your fears, and all the things that you want to let go of. Right now, you can make the decision to slowly release your grip. Release every balloon and everything they represent and imagine them floating out of your life. Allow yourself to see them float away and feel the sense of freedom as everything you released becomes smaller and smaller as it floats completely out of your life.

| 13 |

THE SLED PRINCIPLE

HAVE YOU EVER watched kids sledding in the snow? The excitement of being the first to master the biggest hill. It's as if they inherently understand the importance of being a trailblazer and having the opportunity to provide an incredible path for not only themselves but also for those who come after them. As a trail blazer, the first few rides may be a bit slower as you break new ground and create a new path.

In life, it can be the same way. When you dare to be a trailblazer, it might take a little longer as you forge a new path. Creating a new path takes more time and patience, but it will be worth it as you prepare the way for yourself and others. When you are willing to take risks, you can literally remove barriers and obstacles for yourself and for others who may follow your lead.

You May Need a Push to Get Going

Sometimes you need a little push to get going. You must push yourself or surround yourself with people who are willing to help you and give you an extra push. Sometimes when sledding, you get to the top of the hill, and you are ready to take the plunge, but the sled won't move unless you give yourself a push or have someone push you. In life, it is not much different, you must learn to push yourself if you want to get moving forward in the right direction, and you have to surround yourself with people who will push you to do better. If you get to a point where you feel like you can't push yourself, you must be willing to ask for a little help.

It Becomes Faster and Easier With Repetition

Often when you go sledding, the more times you ride the trail, the faster and further you will go. The repetition has a way of making the path smoother and causes the sled to go faster and further. The same is often true in life. If you stick with it, you will get better, and you will be able to go faster and further than you ever imagined to achieve your goals.

Climbing to the Top Is Exhausting

To enjoy sledding, you must first climb to the top of a hill. It can be exhausting climbing to the top, but you must be willing to climb because the fun begins when you get to the top. Sledding is about balancing work and play. It is about working hard and then enjoying your hard work. You can't sled on a flat surface so first, you must put in the hard work, tackle the challenging hills, and exert some energy. After you put in the work, you can enjoy the ride.

The same is true in life, it can be exhausting to climb your way to the top. It can be scary facing the hills and mountains in your life, but you must have courage and patience and learn to embrace the ups and downs. If you are facing a mountain in your life, keep climbing. Your freedom and enjoyment is waiting for you at the top of your mountain. Success in life is about conquering the mountains, working hard, and then taking time out to enjoy all your hard work.

You May Find Yourself Back at the Bottom

Sledding involves climbing to the top only to find yourself back where you started. Sometimes life is the same way. You may climb to the top only to find yourself back at the bottom. Sometimes starting a new job or a new career field feels like starting back at the bottom again. Sometimes the loss of a loved one or a failed relationship can feel like you are starting back over at the bottom, but just like sledding, keep climbing. Life is full of ups and downs, enjoy the ride, and when you find yourself at the bottom, pick yourself up and keep climbing.

| 14 |

THE MAPLE SYRUP PRINCIPLE

WHAT DO YOU eat for breakfast? Imagine indulging yourself and starting your day with the heavy fragrance of warm maple syrup, drizzled over fluffy pancakes, or Belgium waffles, and your favorite cup of coffee or tea.

The Process Makes the Difference

Real maple syrup goes through an extensive process to release the wholesome sweetness hidden inside a tree. The same is true in life; there is goodness on the inside of you, but you must go through the process. Just like syrup, life can be sticky and life can be sweet, but don't allow the sticky times to keep you stuck in negativity and thoughts of self-defeat. Instead, embrace the process, be patient, and allow the sweetness, kindness, and goodness to pour out of you, making your life and the world around you just a little bit sweeter.

Stress Produces Authenticity

The harvesting and production of real maple syrup takes time and patience, and there is not much syrup produced in fair weather. It is the stress put on the trees and the rough conditions that produce the authentic sweetness hidden inside the tree.

When you face stress and rough patches in life, it might be difficult to be kind and allow the sweetness to flow from inside of you. But you need to see the process through. The stress and pressure you experience is simply part of the process, and the rough conditions are what produce authenticity inside of you. As with syrup, your character, your strength, and your resilience are produced during rough conditions. You can allow the stress in your life to produce compassion, sweetness, and goodness inside of you that you pour out into the world to make a difference.

You May Not See What Is Happening on the Inside

You can walk through the forest and not even know what is going on inside the trees. On the inside, there is a process happening that will produce sweet sap that can be poured out to make valuable maple syrup.

The same is true in life. You may walk past people and not know what they are experiencing on the inside. In fact, you may walk through life and fail to see that the struggles and battles you are facing are simply part of the process that is working on the inside of you. A process that is strengthening you and preparing you for the greatness that is going to flow out of you and make a difference in the world. When you are committed to personal development and constant growth, there is power and goodness waiting to pour out of you from the inside. Just because you do not see the greatness pouring out of your life right now, be patient. Like maple syrup, the harvesting and production of real authentic success is a process that takes time and patience.

There is Value in Authenticity

Real natural maple syrup is not cheap. It costs a great deal more than the imitation because there is value in the real thing. You are most valuable when you are your true self, perfectly imperfect and authentic.

It is the extensive process that makes the difference in the quality of maple syrup. Going through the process of stress and rough conditions does not diminish the value of the maple syrup, it is the process that separates the imitation syrup from the real maple syrup.

The same is true in life, every experience, everything you have been through and will go through is making you more authentic, valuable, and stronger. Your past, your struggles, and trials are not diminishing your value; they are making you more valuable.

Like syrup, life can be sticky and life can be sweet but you must not allow the sticky times to keep you stuck in negativity, fear, and thoughts of self-defeat. Instead, allow the process and everything you face to refine you, so your authenticity, goodness, and sweetness can pour out of you, making the world around you just a little bit sweeter.

| 15 |

THE BUBBLE PRINCIPLE

IMAGINE BEAUTIFUL SOAPY bubbles glistening and shimmering as they swirl, dance, and float gently and freely in the air, but then in the blink of an eye, the bubbles vanish.

Life is Fragile

Life can be as fragile as a beautiful bubble. Tomorrow is not promised. Life is too short to stress and worry about the troubles of the day. Just like bubbles in a tub, you must know when it is time to pull the plug. You need to let all the stress, worries, and rubbish flow down the drain, so you can live a bubbly life full of enthusiasm, positivity, and success.

Make Time for Rest and Renewal

Bubbles can be a great reminder that you must make time for rest and renewal. Every day you have a chance for a fresh start. Life can be full of challenges, and a bubble bath can signify renewal and a fresh start. A bubble bath can be a great way to wash away the tension, stresses and worries of the day. A few minutes in the tub may help you clear your mind and relax your body. The same way you pull the plug and let all the water drain from the tub, you can pull the plug on all the things that drain you.

Maybe you don't take baths, but you can take a hot shower and make time to relax and release any tension, nonsense, drama, and troubles from your life. Make time every day to celebrate your life. Make everyday a fresh start and decide to live a bubbly life full of excitement, zeal, and positivity.

Be Bubbly and Confident

Do you know anyone with a bubbly personality? Have you ever been told you have a bubbly personality? Bubbles are calming and enjoyable, and someone who is confident, enthusiastic about life and has a positive attitude is said to have a bubbly personality. Bubbles signify peace, relaxation, and prosperity. Bubbles are comforting, whether in a bath, at the bottom of a waterfall, or bubbles blown from a child's bubble wand.

Having a bubbly personality is having a positive vibe, being optimistic and seeing the good in everyone and every situation. It is focusing on the brighter side of things and being passionate about living life. It is relishing each moment and making a difference in the world around you.

Forgive Yourself and Others

Living a bubbly life means you need to forgive yourself and forgive others. You must let go of anger, hatred, negativity, jealousy, and anything that weighs you down. Life is too short to hold grudges and walk around mad all the time. Forgiveness is freeing and will remove the heaviness from your life, so you can live a carefree and unencumbered life like a beautiful bubble.

Don't Let Anyone Burst Your Bubble

People will always find something negative to say, but do not allow people to burst your bubble and stop you from being happy or satisfied with your life. If want to have a bubblier personality, you must start with being positive. Being positive requires, looking for and finding the positive things in life. It means thinking positive, believing positive, speaking positive, and surrounding yourself with positive people, content, and ideas. Being positive requires intentionally believing the best, looking for the best, and finding the positive perspective in every situation. Believe in yourself, believe the best, believe you can, believe that you will. Believe that the best is always yet to come. You can choose to be bubbly, optimistic, and courageous. You can be anything you desire when you choose to believe.

| 16 |

THE FIRE PRINCIPLE

WHAT LIGHTS YOUR fire? What are you passionate about? Fire can be both useful and dangerous. Fire can be used for cooking your food, keeping you warm, and providing light, and a host of other benefits. But uncontrolled fire is the exact opposite. Uncontrolled fire can be extremely dangerous and even deadly. It can cause pain and suffering and destroy anything it encounters.

The same is true for the way you choose to live your life. You can use the fire inside of you to be useful and provide value to the world. You can use your gifts and talents to inspire and help others, or you can live a life that is reckless, harmful, and blazing out of control causing pain and suffering, and destroying anything that comes into your path. As you go through life avoid people who are living reckless lives, blazing out of control, and destroying everything they encounter. Choose to be a person who uses your internal flame and your passions to bring warmth, love, and light to the world around you.

Find the Spark

Lighting a fire begins with a small spark, but sometimes getting the fire started is the hardest part. You must find the spark that will cause the fire to begin to burn. When wood is exposed to the elements, rain, and harsh weather, it is hard for it to catch fire, and you must nurture the sparks to get a real fire burning.

The same is true in life, finding your spark that lights the fire in you can be the hardest part in living a life you love. Finding the thing that you love, your passion, the thing you believe you were made to do can sometimes be a challenge.

There may be times in life when you face difficult seasons with harsh experiences, and it can feel like your spark is gone. Whether you lose your spark in your personal life, professional life, or spiritual life, you must take time to rekindle the fire.

Rekindle the Fire

One way you can rekindle the fire is by asking inspiring questions, like what makes you feel most fulfilled in life? What would you do if failure was not an option? What are you grateful for? What do you need to change in your life?

If you had only a week to live, what would you spend your time doing? It only takes one small spark to turn into a powerful fire. The same is true in life. Take the time to recognize and nurture the small sparks in your life. No matter how small the spark, you can fan the flame and begin to live a life on fire. Living a life on fire is about living a life filled with passion. It is living a significant life that makes a difference because you follow your dreams, do what you love, love what you do, and live each and every day to the fullest.

Keep the Fire Burning

You must actively watch a fire to keep it burning. You must pay attention to small changes and be ready to add new stuff to the fire before it starts to dwindle. The same is true in life. To live a life on fire requires active observation so you can decide if life has lost its spark. Has the meaning of your life been lost to the daily grind of living? Is the spark waning in your personal, professional, or spiritual life? If you feel like something might be missing, it may be time to reignite the spark and get a fire re-burning in your life.

In your personal life, you might get the spark back by spending time alone in nature, or reconnecting with your spouse, children or friends. You may choose to add value to the community through volunteering or exercising your faith. In your professional life, you may find a new career, start a business, or seek out meaningful work that will provide benefits to others and provide value to your organization and industry.

Always keep your eyes on the fires burning in your life. The dual nature of fire requires you to always monitor the flames. If you become complacent the flames could fizzle out or get out of control and cause destruction and even death. Always tend to the fires in your life to ensure they provide warmth, light and positive benefits to your life and the atmosphere around you.

| 17 |

THE NAIL PRINCIPLE

BUILDING A LIFE you desire, requires having the right tools. Nails are used in many projects. Nails are used for building things and joining things together, but nails are of no value when they are simply sitting in the box. The value of nails comes from using them for their designed purpose. The same is true in life, you will live a fulfilled life and bring the most value to the world when you have the courage to step outside of the box and accomplish the purpose you were designed for.

Get the job done Quicker and Easier

When you operate in your areas of strength you can get the job done quicker and with more ease. There are many different types of nails, and they all have different purposes. You must select the nail with the right characteristics and strengths to ensure you get the job done effectively. The wrong nail can result in a weak connection or even damage to the material you are joining together.

The same is true in life. You have a purpose in life, and you have unique gifts and talents. When you choose to focus on your strengths it gets you closer to understanding and appreciating your unique gifts, talents, and your specific purpose in life.

When you find yourself in the wrong career, or a wrong personal or professional relationship it can be like using the wrong nail for the job. You may feel a weak connection, or the connection may be damaging or hurtful.

If you find yourself in an incompatible situation, it does not mean there is a problem with you; it simply means you are designed for a different purpose. Sometimes you must remove the wrong nails and start over to make sure what you are building is strong, stable, and built to last.

Avoid Getting Rusty

Nothing remains the same. The world is constantly changing, and you must be willing to grow and change if you want to remain relevant. You must constantly sharpen your skills and learn new things. You must take the time to master and maintain mastery of new skills. Once you learn a skill, you must continually practice those skills to avoid getting rusty. Like a nail if you get rusty, it will make it harder to get the job done. In many professions there is an annual requirement to take training and refreshers because without it, you may become rusty. When you are rusty, you may fail to get the job done properly, safely, or in a timely manner. Are there areas in your life that you have allowed yourself to get rusty?

Don't Get Bent out of Shape

Are you an impatient person? Do you have a temper that sometimes causes you to get bent out of shape? The problem with getting bent out of shape is that it can be hard if not impossible to fulfill your purpose. If you have ever tried to hammer a nail, and it got bent out of shape, you know how frustrating and difficult it is to complete a project with a bent nail.

The same is true in life, if you get bent out of shape and act in anger, impatience, jealousy, unforgiveness, or ungratefulness, it will be harder to fulfill your purpose and can even make it impossible.

If you feel like something is holding you back from fulfilling your purpose, check your attitude. Maybe you are a little bent out of shape. You must learn to control your emotions and control your thoughts. Getting bent out of shape can hinder your progress and growth. A bent nail is unreliable, unstable, and insecure. Avoid people who are always getting bent out of shape. They are unreliable, unstable, and insecure. They will cause you frustration and hinder your progress.

Avoid getting bent out of shape. Getting bent out of shape can jeopardize your health, relationships, business growth, and your ability to get things done. You can avoid getting bent out of shape by paying attention to the thoughts you dwell on and how you interpret situations. Life is not what happens to you but rather how you respond. How do you respond when things do not go your way? Do you find yourself getting bent out of shape, or do you stay strong and resilient, so you can get the job done?

| 18 |

THE INSTRUMENT PRINCIPLE

HAVE YOU EVER tuned in to a radio show, and for a few minutes you became introspective because the lyrics were so relatable? You felt so in tune with the words, it was as if you could have written them yourself? An indescribable feeling comes over you as you realize you are not alone and someone else knows exactly how you are feeling. It's exciting, comforting, and reassuring.

Get in Tune

Being in tune is not only about music, and being in tune is not only for musicians. A tune is a song, it's a melody, but it is also a feeling that things are right. In tune can mean vibrating on the same frequency, resonating and being in harmony. It can mean having a good understanding of yourself, someone, or something else. It can mean sharing common interests and sharing similar attitudes and beliefs.

Sometimes you may go through life disconnected from your inner self, looking for someone else to complete the lyrics to your song and bring harmony to your life, but life is like a symphony, and you have your own part to play. If you don't like the rhythm and tune coming from your life, understand you must first be in tune with yourself because one out of tune instrument can ruin a perfect tune.

Get in tune with your inner self. When you learn how to carry your own tune, and when you learn what makes your heart sing, you will discover the stress-relieving power of living in harmony, and you will play your own song and sing the song of your heart in perfect tune.

The Perfect Harmony

When you are in tune with your authentic self you will feel inner peace, contentment, and satisfaction. There is joy and gratitude. Your priorities are clear, and things flow naturally. You are enthusiastic, and there is a sense of freedom. You can get things done without procrastinating. You feel tranquil and calm and aligned with your purpose.

When you are in tune with who you are, your thoughts line up with your actions and you feel fully alive. On the other hand, when you are out of tune with yourself, you may feel anger, stress, negativity, doubt, procrastination, self-defeat, and frustration. You may have this indescribable feeling that something is just not right. You may feel like you are always searching for answers, and your efforts may seem like a struggle. You may have a lack of trust for yourself and others, and you may question your own value and worth. You may even begin to experience feelings of tension, a lack of energy, and a feeling of hopelessness.

Getting in Tune Requires Time and Attention

Staying in tune requires time and energy. If an instrument sits around neglected or gets knocked around, it will become out of tune. Just like an instrument, you must be intentional about getting in tune and remaining in tune. In the same way, if you neglect the relationship with yourself and others, you can become out of tune.

Getting your life in tune with yourself and others requires consistent time and attention. It requires turning off technology, avoiding multitasking and listening with your ears and your heart.

You will know when your life is in tune because being in tune feels right. When you are in tune with your family and friends you may say things at the same time or think similar thoughts. You may laugh at the same jokes. You might call or send a text at the same time, and you will know exactly what to say at the right time. But being out of tune is like playing on different pages of music; it just does not produce the same harmony.

Living a positive life is about positive vibrations. Living in harmony and being in tune. When stringed instruments are in tune, the strings vibrate at the same rate to produce a rich distinct note, but when they are out of tune, there is a wavering sound that distorts the note, creating an uncomfortable sound. The sounds are out of tune and rather than being on one accord, the sounds begin to compete.

The same is true in life, when you are out of tune, there is struggle and strife and there is a wavering and shakiness in relationships, creating uncomfortable sounds and conversations. There is competition rather than collaboration. Being in tune starts with you. It begins with knowing that you are like an instrument, and every instrument has a valuable part to play in creating an impeccable tune and melody.

Tuning and Retuning is Critical for Harmony

Even the most expensive instruments played by the greatest musicians must be tuned before they are played. The beauty of an orchestra is the power of different instruments coming together to create a unified song. Every instrument creates a different sound, and a unique expression, but when an orchestra is in tune, the music is complementary, and it all fits together.

In life, it is the same way, when you are in tune with your family and friends, co-workers, and community, you can work together in unity. When you remove the strife and competition and appreciate the beauty of working together in harmony, you can contribute to making the sweetest music ever. Everyone brings a different voice and unique way of expressing themselves, but a unified approach can lead to a louder, stronger, and more powerful melody.

When people stop playing together, everyone suffers and even the music of the best players can get lost in the chaos and noise. You will know you are out of synch, because there is tension and uneasiness.

Musicians retune their instruments on a regular basis. But what about you? If you were an instrument, how might people describe the music coming from your life? Would they describe it as loud, soft, harsh, gentle, warm, dark, mellow, or piercing?

You are like a beautiful instrument, and it is your job to ensure you stay in tune and make beautiful music that is not too sharp and not too flat. You can tune and retune your life by watching what you think and speak. Avoid using words that are so sharp they cut and hurt yourself and others. Avoid things and people that drain you and cause you to become flat, deflated, tired, unengaged, and distracted. Fill your mind with harmonious thoughts, ideas, and beliefs, so you can remain in tune with positivity and strength.

You Have a Part to Play

When you meet someone new, do you notice the similarities or differences? Do you value differences, or do you fear them and despise them? What if life is like a huge orchestra, and everyone has a role to play? What if every instrument and all its uniqueness is seen as valuable and essential to create the perfect song and harmony? What if the whole world worked together to make a unified song with a magnificent melody? Do you think we could make the world an even better place if we realized that we are the instruments, and the beauty of the songs depends on each instrument playing their part in unity and on one accord? You have a part to play. What are you doing every day to stay in tune so you can make a difference and create a melody that will make the whole world want to sing and dance together?

| 19 |

THE TABLE PRINCIPLE

PEOPLE CAN BE like tables. They can be solid and strong, or they can be unbalanced and unstable. If you were a table how would people describe you? Are you strong, and resilient, or are you unbalanced and insecure?

It is almost impossible for a table to fulfill its purpose if it is shaky and unstable. The same is true in life. It will be difficult for you to achieve your goals and fulfill your purpose if you are shaky, insecure, and self-doubting. The best tables are the ones that are strong enough for you to lean on, hold you up and keep you from falling. Be like a table people love to gather around and surround yourself with people who are balanced, stable and are willing to hold you up and not let you fall.

Relationships Matter

A dining table can symbolize many things for different people. It can be a place where people come together, a place where you celebrate important milestones, share experiences, and create new understandings with great conversation. A table can be a place where you nourish your belly and sometimes even your soul.

A table can have a multitude of uses including bringing people together. The value of the table lies in the relationships, the history, and the memories with the people gathered around the table.

In life, material things are nice, and they make life enjoyable, but like a table, the real value comes from the people you share your life with. It is the people you surround yourself with that bring the value to your life. It is the people you share your love, respect, and meals with at the table that make a table valuable.

Support Helps Provide Balance

The legs on a table are critical to providing support and balance. Support can be defined as help and assistance that makes it possible for something to function or act. Support can also be reinforcement and encouragement. If a table is missing a leg or has a problem with a leg, the table will be off balance. A missing or damaged leg will hinder the table from serving its purpose, and it may cause other people or things to fall and be damaged as a result.

The same is true in life. You cannot depend on people who are insecure, unstable, and unbalanced. You need to have a support system in place to help you and assist you, so you can function and accomplish your purpose. If you find yourself off balance, check your support system. Find solid people you can lean on and depend on to help support you and help you achieve balance in all areas of your life.

| 20 |

THE CLOCK PRINCIPLE

THE RHYTHMIC TICK tock of a clock can be hypnotic when you consider that each tick and each tock is a reminder that every second and every minute of every hour of each day really does matter.

All We Have is Now

There are moments in life when time seems to matter even more. There are difficult times when you may feel like one minute is the longest minute of your life. And then there are beautiful times where you might find yourself wishing the moment could last forever. There will be other times when you may wish you could turn back the hands of time. Sometimes there are moments where you might wish you could make time stand still, and sometimes you might wish you could speed up time and move forward.

The reality is you can only live in the moment. You cannot slow down, speed up, pause, or stop time. You can only live in the here and now and enjoy every second you have. Living in the moment is not about failing to plan for the future, but it is about living and being present right now. Living in the moment is learning from the past and not worrying about tomorrow, but simply enjoying and being grateful for the gift of the present.

Small Consistent Action Leads to Big Changes

One of the amazing things about a clock is it demonstrates the tremendous power of small consistent action. The consistent movement of that small or sometimes even invisible second hand leads to changes in the second, minute, and hours, and ultimately in the day's weeks, months, and years!

The same is true in life, it is the small consistent actions you take that will lead to big achievements and success. If you want to achieve success in any area, start with small consistent efforts. The reverse is also true, small negative actions consistently done over time can lead to a disastrous and miserable life.

Time is a great reminder that every minute is brand new, and you can invest it however you choose, but once time has passed, it is gone forever. You never get that time back, so choose to invest every second of your life wisely.

Time Is Slipping Away

Have you ever used a timer or stop watch? Maybe you have used an oven timer, microwave, or timer on your phone without realizing you are literally watching time slip away. Time does not cease to exist or stop moving simply because the clock battery dies or the electricity goes out. The same is true in life, time existed before you and will continue after you are gone. Your job is to appreciate time and learn to use it fully. Learning to budget your time is more valuable than learning to budget your money, because once time is gone, you cannot make more. You must decide each and every day how to invest the time you are given, so you can get the biggest return on your investment.

If you pay attention, you will realize how fast time really goes by and how much can change in the blink of an eye. You never know what time has in store for you or when it will run out, so you must have the courage to love hard and live fully.

| 21 |

THE BAGGAGE PRINCIPLE

IMAGINE GOING ON the expedition of a lifetime. The journey you have always dreamed of! But what if life is the journey? One of the things you must do when you travel is pack your baggage. Anyone who is moving and fully experiencing the journey of life will carry some baggage. Baggage is inevitable for people on the move. People who are not going anywhere, playing it safe, and staying in the same place do not have baggage.

Sometimes the more you move the more baggage you have, and the bigger and heavier it will become. But do not beat yourself up for having baggage. Your baggage is simply evidence that you are not stationary or stagnant. You are on the move; you are taking chances, living, moving, and growing through the amazing journey of life.

Carry it or Check it

When it comes to baggage, you can carry it, or you can check it. When you arrive at an airport, you are given the option to check your baggage or carry it with you. It is likely you will choose to carry what you need and check what will weigh you down.

The same is true in life. You may think of baggage as all the negative memories and experiences, but when you pack your baggage for vacation, you pack the things you need. You pack the necessities and the niceties.

In a similar way, in life you can choose to carry what you need for your journey, the positive, empowering, healthy and happy memories. But you must check the bags where you have stored all of your bad memories, hurts, fears, insecurities, all of the negativity, hatred, jealousy, and fear. Your life is the journey of a lifetime, so keep your baggage packed with the things that are helpful and not harmful and the things you need to make this an amazing journey.

Baggage Can Get in the Way

When you ride on a plane, the stewardess will tell you that during take-off and landing, you must store your baggage because it is a safety hazard to yourself and others. The same is true if you are taking a road trip or driving a vehicle. Keeping your baggage in your lap while driving will get in the way. You may not be able to see clearly over the baggage, and your baggage could hinder your ability to steer the steering wheel and go in the direction you desire.

The same is true in life, when you fail to check your baggage, it can be a hazard to your health and success. It can weigh you down, and it may hinder your vision. You may not be able to steer in the direction of your dreams, and you may not be able to make the moves you desire because you have too much baggage in your lap.

You are only designed to carry so much and trying to carry everything is unsafe. Carrying around the social and emotional baggage, the memories, expectations, and experiences from your past can be dangerous. Sometimes it's the guilt, regret, negative self-talk, and beliefs that weigh you down, and hinder you from moving forward. If you are carrying around too much baggage, it can begin to pile up so high that it can obstruct your view of a brighter future. Heavy baggage will not only slow you down, but if you carry the same baggage around for too long, it will eventually become old and stinky.

Keep an Eye on Your Baggage

When you check your bags at the airport, the attendant will ask if anyone else has packed your bag, or if you have left your bag unattended at any time. The reason they ask this question is because not everyone has good intentions, and if you are not vigilant, someone may drop harmful or dangerous items into your baggage that could cause catastrophic damage.

The same is true in life. Your mind, body, and soul is like baggage. It is where you carry your valuables, your souvenirs, your good and bad memories, and experiences from your journey. You must be vigilant about what you allow other people to pour into the baggage of your mind, body, and soul. Not everyone has good intentions, and they may fill your life with negative material, thoughts, and beliefs that could cause catastrophic damage to your self-esteem, self-respect, and self-image. Choose carefully what you allow people to place into your life and make a decision to not carry around garbage in your baggage.

Know Where You are Heading

To pack appropriately for your destination, you must know where you are heading. If your baggage is full of negativity, hatred, fear, and laziness, but your desired destination in life is success, you will need to unpack and repack positivity, hard work, motivation, and integrity. There will be times when you may need to pack and repack but knowing where you are heading can help you avoid carrying excess baggage with items that you do not need, or items that will slow you down and hinder you from reaching your destination.

Baggage Comes with a Cost

Too much baggage comes with a cost. It can impact your experiences and the experiences of the people around you. Have you ever gone to the airport and one of your bags was overweight? This happened on one of our family trips. When we got to the airport, one of the bags was overweight. The attendant told us we had to either pay a fee or balance out the items among other bags. We decided to distribute the items among the other bags rather than pay the overweight fee. This experience was a powerful reminder that in life, when your baggage becomes too heavy, you have three choices. You can let some things go, you can pay the price and continue to carry the heavy load, or you can ask others to help you lighten your load.

The same concept can be applied to a road trip. Have you ever taken a road trip and had too much baggage in the vehicle? It can slow down the journey and everyone in the vehicle is uncomfortable because there is less room to stretch! The same is true in life, when you carry too much baggage, you can make your life and the lives of those around you uncomfortable. You don't have room to stretch and grow, and you can also hinder the growth of the people close to you.

Every day as you move though life, you must remember that too much baggage comes with a cost, and you must make a habit to regularly check, pack, and unpack your baggage. You must unpack all the things that weigh you down like, anger, unforgiveness, jealously, and hatred, and replace them with faith, gratitude, determination, forgiveness, and love.

| 22 |

THE POTS AND PANS PRINCIPLE

POTS AND PANS are the most frequently used items in the kitchen, but pots and pans have a greater purpose than simply being used to prepare food. They are also containers that hold items that can be served to feed, nourish, encourage, and sustain life. In life, it is the same way, you have a greater purpose. You contain gifts inside of you that can be served, distributed, delivered, presented, and given as a contribution to the greater good, to help others, and to make a difference in the world.

Know Your Purpose

Pots and pans come in a variety of shapes, sizes, and colors, but each pot is designed for a specific purpose and use. In the same way, people come in a variety of shapes, sizes, and colors, yet each and every person is designed for a specific purpose.

A professional chef knows exactly which pots and pans are needed to get the job done efficiently and effectively, but a novice chef may use the wrong pots and pans and question why their meal was not satisfying.

In life, it can be the same way. You must be a professional when it comes to cooking up a life you love. Professionalism is about setting high standards and holding yourself accountable for your thoughts, words, and actions in every aspect of your life. Being a professional will help you understand your purpose and the best way to get things done. When you do not know your purpose, you may find yourself in the wrong career, in the wrong relationship, or the wrong community, being used to do things that are not aligned with your true purpose. You must know your specific purpose, or you may find yourself wondering why your life is not satisfying.

Your Aroma and Your Vibe

Have you ever noticed that whatever you put in your pots and pans will create an aroma that saturates the air? Sometimes it's a pleasant fragrance, and sometimes it's an awful stench. The same is true in life; your mind and your life can be like pots and pans. Whatever you pour into your life will create an aroma that will saturate the environment around you.

Your aroma is like your vibe, if you pour positive, faith-filled, success-driven thoughts into your mind and surround yourself with upbeat, caring, hardworking, honest, mature, and thoughtful people, your life will give off a sweet-smelling fragrance and a positive uplifting vibe. But if you pour garbage, negative, and destructive thoughts of failure into your mind and surround yourself with dishonest, selfish, grouchy, and lazy people, it can lead to a foul aroma, a very stinky attitude and a repulsive negative vibe.

Pay Attention to the Inside

Have you ever left something unattended in a pot on the stove? Maybe you got distracted or sidetracked while you were cooking. You might have figured out really quick that you must always pay attention to what is taking place on the inside. If you fail to pay attention to what is happening on the inside, it can lead to disaster. It can get messy if everything from the inside transfers to the outside. You may find yourself having to pour the contents down the drain, or dispose of it in the garbage.

The same is true in life, you can't ignore what is taking place on the inside. You must be aware of what is on the inside because eventually whatever is on the inside will spill over to your outside life. If you don't pay attention to what is on the inside, your life can get messy. You may find yourself wasting your life away, or throwing your gifts, talents, and your dreams down the drain.

Inspect the Core

You must inspect the core of the pots and pans. The appearance of pots and pans will grow dull over time, but if you fail to pay attention to the inside and the core of the pan is damaged, there is a serious problem. The outside of a pot or a pan can look shiny and bright, but if there is a crack or damage to the inside, it must be addressed, because internal damage can cause serious problems.

The same is true in life. It is not merely about your physical appearance. Sometimes the circumstances of life can dull your enthusiasm. You may walk around looking shiny, happy, and bright on the outside, but on the inside, you may feel broken and hurt. If you have unresolved issues on the inside, address them immediately or they may impact all areas of your life.

You must pay attention to the condition of your insides, your core. Do not spend all your time and attention on your outside appearance because with time, you will grow older on the outside. But your heart is at the core of who you are, and if there is an issue with the core, then there is a real problem that must be addressed.

When the inside of a pot is damaged, anything coming from the pot could be toxic and harmful. The same is true in life. You will produce based on what is on the inside. If your mind and heart is full of damaging thoughts and beliefs, then the things being released from you can become damaging and toxic to yourself and others.

Conduct Regular Inspections

Pots and pans must be cleaned and inspected regularly to insure there is no internal damage, and nothing is left stuck on the inside that could cause harm.

The same is true in life. You cannot ignore what is happening on the inside. You must inspect and clean your mind and heart regularly and make sure there is no internal damage. You need to make sure there is nothing stuck on the inside that can cause harm and damage and keep you from loving and living life fully. You must take time to remove the residue from those simmering negative thoughts, those harmful feelings, and any unforgiveness, blame, jealousy, and anger so that it does not get stuck on the inside, leaving you paralyzed, numb, and unable to move forward in life.

Finish What You Start

You must finish what you start. Once you put items in the pots and pans, you must either cook them or you risk having them go to waste. An unfinished meal can leave you feeling unsatisfied, like something is missing, and an undercooked meal can make you extremely sick.

The same is true in life. Those unfinished projects, unfinished goals, and dreams, those forgotten new year's resolutions, that unused gym membership, or that lingering situation that still needs closure can leave you feeling unsatisfied, like something is missing in life. When you do not finish what you start, it can make you feel sick; sick and tired with regret and disappointments about what could have and should have been. Are there things that you have been afraid to start or things you neglected to finish? It is never too late. You don't have to live a life of regret; someday is today. Now is the time.

| 23 |

THE POPCORN PRINCIPLE

IMAGINE A BOWL of warm, fresh, fluffy, buttery popcorn. Popcorn can be a yummy treat, but popcorn can also teach the unchanging principle of seed, time, and harvest.

From Your Purpose to Your Potential

Popcorn is a great example of what it looks like to go from your purpose to your potential. When you put a bag of popcorn in the microwave, it is not a bag of popcorn yet, it is simply a bag of popcorn seeds. They are seeds of possibility that can grow to fulfill their true potential.

The same is true in life. You possess within you seeds of potential, but there is a process to move from your purpose into your potential.

Do Not Compare Your Progress

Everything happens at the designated time. Popcorn seeds do not achieve their potential at the same exact time. Even when seeds are in the exact same pot or bag, they all pop at different rates.

The same is true in life, don't compare yourself to others. You may be in the same family, same community, same company, on the same team, but do not compare yourself to anyone else. Don't worry if it looks like others are popping off and achieving their success quicker than you. There is no way to know which seeds will pop first or which seeds will pop at all.

The same is true in life. You do not know which seeds will produce the results you desire or when you will see the seeds of success pop in your life, but you must see the process through. You must continue planting seeds of hard work, commitment, gratitude, and kindness consistently until you accomplish your purpose and reach your full potential.

Your Ending Can Look Different Than Your Beginning

It does not matter if you had a bad beginning. Your ending can look drastically different than your beginning. You might be thinking things don't look so great right now, but it doesn't matter what things look like right now, because tomorrow can look drastically different. You need to understand that your beginning does not dictate your ending.

Popcorn kernels start out plain and hard. They appear dry and useless at the beginning of the process, and yet they transform into beautiful, fluffy delicious treats once they are put in the right environment and go through the process.

The same is true in life. As you go through the process of fulfilling your purpose, your life will not look the same. When you position yourself in the right environment, one that is positive and conducive to productivity and growth, you can walk in your purpose and reach your full potential.

Practice Patience

Having patience and waiting can be one of the hardest things to do in life. There is a principle of seed, time, and harvest, and the formula requires first planting the seed, then nurturing it patiently over time, and then finally you will reap your harvest. Maybe you are great at planting the seeds and expecting the harvest but find yourself struggling with patiently waiting to see the harvest manifest.

Popcorn provides a powerful example of the principle of seed, time, and harvest. Have you ever noticed when you put a bag of popcorn seeds in the microwave, nothing happens at first? But with a little bit of time, the pressure builds up, and the seeds begin to pop. However, it is not just one big pop. You must be patient and allow each kernel to transform into its full potential so you can enjoy it for its purpose.

The same is true in life. There are times when you might feel like nothing is happening and sometimes you feel the pressure building up, but it still looks like nothing is happening. Be encouraged, like popcorn with time, you will slowly begin to achieve your potential and walk into your purpose.

Grow Through the Pressure

You may face challenges and struggles in your life. Sometimes the pressure may seem like too much to handle. Like popcorn seeds, sometimes transforming seeds of potential to their purpose requires intense heat, struggle, and challenges. If you are making popcorn, and you take them out of the heat too soon, they will stop popping. You hinder the transformation process. Some of the kernels will not be able to reach their full potential.

The same is true in life. Are there seeds you destroyed because you gave up too soon? Are there things you potentially missed out on because you gave up just before your seeds of potential began to pop? Are you walking in your purpose, or are you walking around with unharvested seeds of potential?

Don't be afraid of the preparation stage. When the heat is on, stay in the process. Use the heat to develop and expand yourself, so each positive seed you have planted can begin to pop, and you can begin to move from your potential and begin living out your purpose.

| 24 |

THE ALEXA PRINCIPLE

ARE YOU FAMILIAR with Alexa? Alexa is a convenient and handy virtual personal assistant that can listen to your voice commands and respond with appropriate actions to help you get a job done.

A Positive Energy Source is Critical

Without energy and power, Alexa is useless and will not be able to fulfill her purpose. The same is true in life, you must take care of your mind, body, and soul so that you have energy and power to fulfill your purpose.

You can increase your energy level by eating healthy foods, exercising, seeking balance in work and play, and tending to your mental and spiritual health.

You must figure out what you can plug into that will energize you and give you the power and energy you need to be your best each day. Do what invigorates you and remove those things that disconnect you from your power and drain your energy. Things like negative thinking, negative people, worry, lack of sleep, people pleasing, clutter, and disorganization. All these things can limit your energy and power and leave you drained and unable to fulfill your purpose.

It's All about Connections

Alexa must be connected. You must connect Alexa to your devices, apps, and programs. Alexa is all about her connections. The right connections enable her to operate at her full capacity. For example, if Alexa is connected to your light switch, you can tell her to turn on the light, but if she is not connected, she will not respond.

The same is true in life, your relationships and connections impact your productivity, energy and everything you think, say, and do. You must surround yourself with people who will support your dreams and help you grow. People who lift you up and inspire you rather than drain you and discourage you. People who make you feel connected, energized, passionate, and confident about who you are and who you can become. Always be mindful about connecting yourself to the right ideas, people, opportunities, resources, communities, and activities, so you can function at your full potential.

Programming Impacts Everything

Alexa operates based on her programming. You have the option to choose what news, music, and information programs you want to receive. Whatever programming you choose will determine what Alexa says and does.

The same is true in life, you must pay attention to what programming you consume. There is a reason why TV shows are called TV programs. Program means to cause someone to behave in a predetermined way. The programs you consume will determine your behavior. They will determine what you think and what you believe. If you are constantly watching and listening to programs full of pessimism, negativity, and hatred, you are being programmed to respond to situations with words of dissatisfaction, negativity, and defeat, but when you watch and listen to inspirational, positive programming, you are being programmed to respond to situations with positivity and words of success.

Your Voice Is Powerful

Alexa is voice-activated. Once she is set up, she learns to recognize your voice. With the power of your words, you can have Alexa deliver messages, songs, products, and more. Your words have tremendous power, and you can use your voice to bring the things you desire into your life. However, your words are so powerful that the opposite is also true. You can bring things you do not want into your life if you are not careful. There have been numerous stories of people getting unwanted products delivered from Amazon because they spoke their words out loud and Alexa heard them and fulfilled their request.

The same is true in life. You must be careful what you speak because you can bring things you do not want into your life with the power of your words.

Your voice is one of the most powerful influences in your life. Humans are the only creatures who use spoken language to communicate. Your voice runs through your mind daily, and you probably believe it! Good or bad, you believe what you tell yourself. Words can fill you with joy, or words can fill you with fear. Words can inspire you or discourage you. Words can be a gift, or words can be a curse. You can brighten someone's day, or you can tear their life apart with mere words. Choose your words carefully.

Words Impact Your Self-Image

Words have creative ability. If someone tells you to imagine you are laying on a warm sandy beach, you can create it and see it in your mind. You might even feel the sand between your toes. Unfortunately, negative words can have the same power and ability.

The words you use and the words you allow others to use about you will impact your self-image. Your self-image is the picture of who and what you believe about yourself. Negative words create an image that becomes crippling and destroys the image you have of yourself. Your self-image can easily be distorted and destroyed by the word's others speak, and the words you choose to believe. Who do you think you are? How do you see yourself? Do you see yourself as beautiful, strong, amazing, unique, and worthy of love and respect, or do you have a negative or damaging image of yourself?

Has anyone including yourself ever spoken words of judgment, and criticism into your life? Negative words can impact your self-image because your mind creates an image of what you hear. The great news is, it works both ways. You can be poised and confident, and your self-image can be positive and optimistic when you speak and listen to positive life-producing words. Do not allow yourself or others to speak negative words over you and make a choice to speak words of encouragement and empowerment into your life and the lives of others every day.

Positive confessions are one way to activate the power of your voice. A positive confession is simply speaking out loud what you want to happen with the expectation and belief that it is possible. Great confessions begin with the words, "I am." Think about it for a moment. It is difficult to feel bad if you are constantly saying, "I am feeling great!" It's hard to be afraid if you continue to tell yourself, "I am brave!" It is hard to feel inadequate if you constantly say, "I am more than enough!" Use the power of your voice to activate the image of yourself and the life you desire to live.

Be Careful What You Respond To

Not only are the words you speak important, but what you respond to is just as critical. Alexa is programmed so that she will only respond to her name. If you call her Alex, Amy, or Al, she is not going to respond, unless you have already programmed her to respond to those names.

In life, it is the same way. Do not let people call you out of your name. Do not allow yourself to become programmed to answer or accept names that do not align with your core beliefs and values. Do not accept being called a loser, failure, disaster, or disappointment. If someone calls you out of your name, just like Alexa, you stand fast. Do not respond, do not answer. Do not allow anyone to alter your programming. Do not accept any unbecoming words or allow negative images to take root in your mind. You are uniquely you, perfectly made in all ways. The fact that you are you is your superpower. There is no one else who has your gifts and talents. Be proud of who you are!

| 25 |

THE WINDOW PRINCIPLE

HAVE YOU EVER sat and stared out of a window? Windows symbolize openness and light, and have been used to represent growth, health, and the courage to change. A window has a distinct ability to be an entrance and an escape. It can let light in while also keeping out dangerous or pesky things. While it has been said the eyes are the windows to the soul, I believe the mind is also like a window.

Your Mind Is like a Window

Did you know you can use your mind to create and change the way you experience situations in life? You may not always be able to change physical situations, but you can use your mind to change the way you feel about a situation. Even though your circumstances may get you down, it is your thoughts about your circumstances that will keep you down. You can use your mind and thoughts to create mental pictures and ideas that refresh and renew your spirit. You can escape the stress of the day by using your mind to think relaxing and positive thoughts. You can create ideas and make decisions that allow you to escape a harmful or dismal situation, and you can improve and expand your life with the power of your mind.

Your mind is so powerful, and like a window, if you allow the light to shine in and restrict the dangerous and pesky things and people from your life, you will have the courage to grow and make positive changes.

Pay Attention to the Blind Spots

When driving a vehicle, the windows are designed to provide you with a 360-degree view, but you must be aware that there are blind spots. Blind spots obstruct a person's view of something. Blind spots are areas where a person is close-minded or lacks understanding. When driving a vehicle, if you plan to move from the left or the right, you must check your blind spots before changing lanes. You must purposely turn your head, move to a new position, and approach things differently to clearly see what is in your blind spot.

The same is true in life. Your mindset is designed to provide you with access to a 365-degree view of the world around you, but you must be aware of your blind spots. Your blind spots are those areas that obstruct your view from seeing things the way they really are because you are closed-minded or lack understanding.

Sometimes your blind spots are those things you don't like about yourself but refuse to acknowledge or the behaviors and attitudes you possess that other people may see but you are not aware of. Just as with driving a vehicle when you take time to uncover your blind spots, it can heighten your sense of awareness and make your journey safer and smoother.

When looking out the windows of your vehicle, your blind spot can cloud your decision. If you do not see a vehicle or anything in your blind spot, you may make a decision that could be harmful or deadly. Sometimes what you do not see is just as impactful as what you do see because both will have an impact on the decisions you make.

The same is true in life, your blind spots can cloud your decisions and what you do not see can make you bias and cause you to take actions that may be dangerous and harmful. Your blind spots in life may hinder your ability to see your goals and dreams clearly. You may fail to see opportunities for change because your vision is distorted by your blind spots.

The View Adds Value

Have you ever noticed that homes with a view cost significantly more than those without a view? Imagine a beautiful home with floor to ceiling windows overlooking a spectacular view, but the windows are so cloudy and foggy that you can't see a thing through them.

In life, it can be the same way. Your mindset gives you the power to change your view and see things from a better perspective. But negative thoughts can be like clouds and fog obstructing your vision and positive view of things.

Now imagine the same beautiful home with brand-new windows restoring the amazing view. An unobstructed view that allows you to see things clearly immediately increases the value of a home.

In life, it is the same way. When you choose to remove the hazy, harmful, destructive thoughts from your life, you will remove the fog that negative thinking creates, and you will be able to see things clearly. When you replace the foggy haze of negative thoughts, it is like looking out a brand-new window. You have a million-dollar view. You can see all the beautiful things surrounding you. You can see the possibilities. You will have a whole new point of view and perspective that will add value and a new appreciation to your life.

The Window Determines What You See

Your mindset is like a window. It determines what you see. You and a neighbor living on the same street can look out a window and see different things because you are looking out different windows.

Imagine you stay at a resort on the first floor, you look out and see a crowded pool. Now imagine you are staying in the same resort on an upper floor. You look out and you see the beautiful blue ocean. It is the same resort, but the window changes the view.

In life, everyone is looking out a different window, but your window will determine how you see people, situations, issues, relationships, and more. You must consider that another person's view is not necessarily wrong, it's just different. Their view is what they see from their window. Sometimes you must take time to see the view from other people's windows, and other times, you must take time to show people the view from your window, so they can understand what you see.

It takes self-awareness, compassion, and empathy to understand that your window is "your" window and not "the" window of life. Your view will make all the difference in the world, so choose to take a positive view in all that you see and do.

| 26 |

THE SNOW PRINCIPLE

FOR SOME PEOPLE, snow is fun and exciting like being inside a life-size snow globe, but for others, snow is simply an unwelcome storm.

Small Storms Can Cause Big Damage

Have you ever considered the size and weight of a single snow flake? They are as light as a feather. But as those flakes continue to fall and accumulate, the wet snow can literally crush plants, trees, and cause a roof to crash in.

Sometimes in life, it can be the same way. You can experience a seemingly small setback or situation in life, but as those small challenges continue to pour into your life, it can be crushing, and if you are not careful, you can be crushed under the weight of them.

No matter how big or strong you are, there may be times when your life is changed in fundamental ways by the pressure of several small problems falling consistently over time.

In life, you must learn to weather the storms and trust that no matter what is falling around you or in your life, it is only for a season. If you are in the middle of a cold wintry storm in life, I have good news, the snow will eventually melt, and with time, there is a change of season. As the snow melts, the plants are nourished and spring back to their former glory, more beautiful and healthier than ever before.

The same is true in life. Nothing stays the same. Seasons change and eventually, the storms of life will pass, but the challenges, the pain, and the disappointments can help you grow so you spring back more beautiful and stronger than ever before.

Storms Can Hinder Your Vision and Slow You Down

Sometimes a storm gets out of control and when it becomes a blizzard, it can hinder your vision and slow you down. You may not be able to see more than a few feet in front of you. You may miss road signs, you may get stuck, you may fall off the road, or you may get lost. You may feel frozen and unable to move completely.

When you face the storms of life, it can be the same way. Sometimes you may get lost. The storms of life can limit your vision of the future. You may be unable to see past the storm to a bright future. You may miss signs and opportunities that can help you get back on track. You may feel frozen and stuck in your problems and unable to move. But just like in a snowstorm, you have options. You don't have to sit and get buried under the weight of the storm; you can find a way to dig your way out, or you can find a safe place to rest and be still until the storm passes.

| 27 |

THE STETHOSCOPE PRINCIPLE

A STETHOSCOPE IS an instrument used to listen to sounds produced within the body, mainly in the heart.

You see when you go to see a doctor, you can look perfectly fine on the outside, but the doctor will use a stethoscope because it can pick up abnormal heart sounds on the inside that may suggest heart disease or failure.

In the same way, sometimes, you may look fine on the outside, but you may be on the verge of emotional sickness or heart failure. Sometimes you need to take time and examine your heart with a metaphorical stethoscope. You need to listen carefully to what is happening on the inside. Like a stethoscope, you must look within to see what cannot be seen from the outside but can only be heard and felt.

Sometimes in life, you may go through situations, and you may get stuck listening to the thoughts in your head and forget to listen to your heart. Has there ever been a time that your mind told you one thing, but your heart told you another thing. One feels right, but one is the most logical. Sometimes you may not move forward with something like a job, a relationship, or decision because your heart is simply not in it. Listening to your heart can be scary sometimes because you want to use your mind to make a safe decision based on the facts. But, if you fail to listen to your heart, you can also fail to leave space for new opportunities.

Your head is often caught up with physical boundaries, but your heart is in touch with your true essence. Sometimes you might think that listening to your heart means being overly sensitive or emotional and subduing all logic and reasoning, but thinking with your heart is being authentic and exercising wisdom, so you can experience calmness and inner peace. Your inner voice speaks through your heart, and when your heart is in it, you will be able to clearly hear the answers to the most important questions in your life.

Heart Disease and Heart Failure

The condition of your heart is affected by the things you ingest with your eyes and ears. Everything you consume will impact your heart. When one is at risk for heart disease or heart failure, the doctor may recommend an adjustment to what they consume and a change in their routine.

To improve and strengthen your heart, the doctor may recommend exercise and movement. The same is true when it comes to your emotional heart. Sometimes you must change the things you are consuming. You may need to change your routine and avoid people who are feeding you harmful, fearful thoughts, negativity, hatred, gossip, and garbage.

You need to exercise your muscles and trust your heart to lead you in the right direction. You need to trust your mind but also have the courage to go where your heart leads you.

| 28 |

THE ELEVATOR PRINCIPLE

ELEVATORS ARE DESIGNED to make it easier to get people and things to different levels. The heavier the load, the more difficult it is to lift something to a higher place. Elevators allow people to carry the heaviest of loads to different levels more efficiently and expediently.

The same is true in life. Life is full of ups and downs, and the heavier your challenges and loads, the harder it can be to lift yourself to a higher place, but your mindset can be like an elevator. The inner workings of your resilient spirit, the courage, and the faith that resides within you will help you go to different levels more quickly and more efficiently.

A positive mindset can make it easier for you to carry heavier loads and climb to higher levels. In the same way, other people can also be like elevators. They can lift you up to higher levels or take you down to rock bottom.

You Can Only Go as High as the Structure

An elevator can only go as high as the building it resides within. The same is true in life. Your mind is like a building. You can only go as high as your mindset allows. You must keep learning, growing, and getting better every single day. You must focus your mind on growth and progress because when you grow, it is like expanding a building. As you grow, you can add more levels and rise to greater heights in all areas of your life.

Enjoy the Journey

When you get on an elevator, it can feel like you are moving so slowly and it is taking forever, but you must learn to enjoy the journey on the way to your destination. You must take time to appreciate your surroundings and enjoy the relationships of the people you meet, no matter how brief the interaction.

People may come and go from your life, sometimes too briefly, but you should enjoy the moments you are given. Understand that many people will climb aboard the same elevator going from one level to the next, but do not get distracted. Not everyone is going to start and finish your journey with you, and that is ok; keep going until you reach your destination.

The same is true in life. Some people who were with you in the beginning will get impatient and leave you alone on your journey. Some people may come into your life for a brief season and not everyone is meant to go with you on your journey. As you ascend to higher levels, there may be people who get tired and do not want to continue moving to the next level, but you must keep going.

Do Not Follow the Crowd

Sometimes you may get on an elevator, and there will be people that got on the elevator after you, but they reach their destination before you. The same is true in life. Do not compare your journey or your destination to anyone else's. Do not get sidetracked or enticed to follow the crowd. Do not be so concerned about others that you find yourself settling for a different level. Stay focused on your journey. The right doors will open, and you will step into the level you have been waiting for. No matter how long it takes be patient and know that your time is coming! Never get discouraged even if you are the first one on and the last one off. It may take you longer to obtain the life you desire. Don't settle; remember, it takes longer to get to the top floor. Be patient, the ascent to the top is not quick or easy, but it is worth the wait. If you do not give up and you keep moving toward your goals every single day, you will eventually arrive.

Close the Door to Get Moving

Like an elevator, sometimes, you must close the door before you can start moving in a new direction. It is only when you close the door to the elevator that it can begin moving in the direction you desire. The elevator will not move with the doors open; it is a hazard, and everyone is at risk of getting hurt. Sometimes you must shut some doors in your life, or you risk hurting yourself and those around you. You must find a way to close some doors and obtain closure from the situations, experiences, people, thoughts, behaviors, and challenges in life that can keep you stuck. You do not have to forget the past; but you must deal with and close the door on the past, so it does not hold you back from reaching higher heights personally and professionally. You must forgive yourself and others and close the door on any pain, guilt, and unforgiveness. You must close the door on negativity, hatred, jealousy, and fear.

It can be hard when it feels like no one understands your dreams and goals or the levels you wish to attain in life, but you must be willing to shut the door on people who are holding you back or hindering you from going to new levels. As hard as it may be sometimes, you must have the courage to close the door and ride alone.

Choose Your Company Wisely

You must choose your company wisely because who you surround yourself with is critical. Like elevators, people can lift you up, support you, and help you reach your destination quicker, or they can keep pushing your buttons and take you up and down on a stressful and emotional ride where you never reach your destination.

Sometimes You Can Feel Trapped

There may be times in life when you feel like you are on an elevator that is completely out of service and not moving at all. Sometimes you can feel like you are trapped and surrounded by strangers, or you might feel like you stuck all alone.

If you ever get trapped in an elevator, do not panic. You must seek help and find a way out. The same is true in life, if you find yourself feeling trapped, where you feel like you are not moving and perhaps you are surrounded by people who are bringing you down, do not panic. Seek help and find a way out. Do all that you can but don't be afraid to ask for help, and when help arrives and that door opens, learn from the experience, move quickly forward, and let that door close behind you.

| 29 |

THE TAPE PRINCIPLE

DO YOU KNOW anyone who is always bringing everyone together, maybe a family member, maybe a friend or co-worker, or maybe it's you? You know the kind of person whose personality is so compassionate and kind, they are always handy to always have around? These types of people are like scotch tape. They can solve problems and help mend tears, and they can make gifts look perfect. They are transparent, and sometimes even invisible because they work behind the scenes, but they always help get the job done.

Find Your Edge

Have you ever lost the end on a roll of tape? It can be extremely frustrating, because you must find the edge before you can continue to use the tape to get your project done.

In life, it is the same way, you need to find your edge to be able to accomplish your projects and goals. When you are searching for the edge on a roll of tape, you may have to go around and around in circles before you find it. Finding your edge in life can be the same way. You may feel like you are going around and around in circles.

The edge of the tape can be right in front of you, but it blends in and becomes stuck. In life, it can be the same way. You must be careful not to simply blend it and get stuck. Do not get stuck thinking and acting like everyone around you. You were created with a unique edge, and you must find it, so you can move forward in the direction of your dreams.

Feel Your Edge

To find the edge on a roll of a tape, you must look very closely, but you must also feel the roll because you will often feel the edge before you see it. Don't skip over any areas because it can be easy to miss, but if you keep looking and feeling for it, it will eventually become apparent.

In the same way finding your personal edge requires a close examination of your life. Do not skip over any areas. Examine your personal, professional, physical, and spiritual life because sometimes you will feel your edge before you see it. You will feel it in your heart, and you will know that you have found your edge. You will feel that this is what you were made for. Keep seeking and be open-minded and eventually, your unique edge will become apparent.

The Edge May Not Be a Straight Line

Finding the edge may not be a straight line. When tape tears, sometimes it tears in a jagged, uneven way. Life can be the same way. Finding your edge is not a clean and flawless process, and it is rarely a straight line. Finding your edge can be more like a messy, squiggly, jagged line that includes missteps, failure, repetition, and loops. You may have to change directions many times but keep going and eventually, you will find your edge.

You Might Not Find It the First Time

When you are looking for the edge of the tape, you may not find it on the first pass. It might feel like you are simply going in circles, but you must keep going and sometimes you will have to switch directions.

The same is true in life, you may not find your edge on the first try, but you must keep trying. Sometimes it will feel like you are simply going in circles, but you must keep searching. There will be times when you must switch directions. You might have to switch careers, go back to school, or start over, but you must keep going and never give up!

What Is Your Edge?

You edge is your unique personal advantage; it is your power. It is what allows you to execute faster and better to get things done. It could be the skills and specialties you have, the positive mindset you possess, your circle of friends, and your network. It could be your kind heart and compassion; it could be your ability to simply listen and encourage others.

Your edge will lead to open doors and opportunities. Your edge will position you to move forward in life, so you can accomplish all your goals and dreams.

Live on the Edge

Living life on the edge can be dangerous yet exhilarating. Being on the edge can make you tense, nervous, and unable to relax. Coming to the edge of your comfort zone is like stepping off the edge of a mountain. It is risky and feels scary.

In yoga, the edge is a beautiful place where you move just beyond your comfort zone and challenge yourself in a healthy way. It's the sweet spot where the body achieves an optimal stretch, and the mind is fully present.

Your edge in life can be the same way. It is that place just beyond your comfort zone. Your edge is the place where you challenge yourself to do something more. It is the place where you challenge yourself to do something unique and different. It is the place where your mind stretches and grows, and you become a better version of yourself.

Embrace the Rough Edges

No one is perfect, and you should embrace your rough edges. It is ok to have some rough edges. When you lose the end of a roll of tape, the end becomes a new beginning. It is the starting point for your next project.

The same is true in life. Your rough edges are not the end of your story. You can use your rough edges, and all your imperfections, faults, and mistakes as a new starting point. Your rough edges are the place where you will put an end to some things and then use the ending as a new beginning. A new starting point to begin again. When you embrace your rough ends, you will realize the end is just a new beginning.

Carefully Choose Your Connections

You must carefully choose who and what you connect yourself to. If you are wrapping a gift and need to remove the tape, you may end up with a piece of paper that refuses to separate itself from the tape. It may leave a tear and emptiness on the gift wrapping paper. You may experience the same thing in life. You may find yourself stuck in the wrong environment, attached to the wrong people, and when you try to remove someone or something from your life, it can get messy, and it can leave you with an emptiness and emotional tears.

You are created with everything you need to hold things together but when you attach yourself to the wrong people and things, it can hinder your ability to hold things together. When tape sticks to the wrong materials, it can collect lint and dirt, and it will hinder its ability to stick, connect and keep things together.

In life, it can be the same way if you find yourself stuck in a bad situation or relationship, health crisis, toxic workplace, or you experience loss or other challenging situations. You might have a hard time holding things together. The challenges of life can leave a residue that make it hard for you to connect with others and keep things together. You may lose your motivation and drive and find it hard to stick to your goals, dreams, good habits, and routines.

Practice Humility and Gratitude

Tape is designed to bring things together and help keep things together, but if tape gets stuck on itself, it becomes useless. It is no longer able to accomplish its purpose and bring other things together because it is stuck on itself.

The same is true in life, if you become stuck on yourself, and lose your humility and gratitude, it may interfere with your ability to fulfil your purpose. It will be difficult for you to make a difference, add significance, and bring other people together because you are too stuck on yourself.

| 30 |

THE DISPENSER PRINCIPLE

DISPENSERS COME IN many different shapes and sizes, but it is not the outside appearance of the dispenser that matters. What matters is what the dispenser holds on the inside.

The same is true in life. It is not about your physical appearance. No matter what you may look like on the outside, it is what you hold on the inside that determines your true value, and it is what is on the inside that will allow you to accomplish your purpose.

Self-Care Is Important

A dispenser is designed to help a container achieve its purpose more efficiently. Without a dispenser, there is nothing to ensure a balanced distribution of the contents of the container. The contents can pour out rapidly which can lead to waste, an empty container, and sometimes a big mess.

You are like a container, and self-care is like a dispenser designed to help you balance how you distribute your time and energy. If you fail to use a metaphorical dispenser, you risk pouring out your energy, power, and motivation too quickly, which can leave you empty and sometimes can cause a big mess in your life.

Preparation is Critical to Accomplish Your Purpose

When you get a new dispenser or add new material to your dispenser, you must first prepare it to accomplish its purpose. It can require a little turning, rotating, and shifting and then once it is in position, you must press and push. The pressing and pushing will build the momentum needed to release what is on the inside.

In the same way, fulfilling your purpose in life requires preparation. You might have to turn away from the familiar and change the way you have always done things. You may have to rotate and move in a new direction physically or mentally. Then you must be ready to press and push forward to reach momentum, so you can release the gifts, talents, and power inside of you to accomplish your purpose.

Remain Fluid

Success is not a fixed, permanent state. It is fluid and ever-changing. Success is a series of choices and actions that you make every single day. In life, you should be very clear on your goals, but you should remain fluid and flexible in how you set out to accomplish them. Life can be full of setbacks and challenges, but you must remain fluid and go with the flow.

Fill up with the Right Stuff

To use a dispenser properly, the container must be full, but it must be full of the items it was made to carry; otherwise, it will not be able to accomplish the purpose it was designed for. If you fill a container full of rocks, they will not be able to flow through the dispenser. They will get stuck and simply take up space in the container, limiting the amount of other material the container can hold.

In life, you are like a container. Your mind, body, and soul are like containers that are filled and emptied by what you spend your time doing. You must pay attention to what you fill your eyes and ears with. You are not designed to be filled with certain things and you are not designed to carry some things, so you must be sure to fill your physical body with the right foods, and keep your mind and spirit full of positive, powerful, faith-filled words and thoughts. When you fill yourself with the wrong things, you limit your ability to carry more of the things you are designed to carry. The things that will allow you to accomplish all your work with passion and excellence.

Refill Constantly

With constant use, a dispenser will need to be refilled on a regular basis. Like a dispenser, you must constantly refill your mind, body, and soul.

When a dispenser is full, the items inside flow out with ease, but as the dispenser gets low, it becomes sluggish and is unable to fulfill its purpose. Even a frantic attempt to push harder will not yield enough output to get the job done. Sometimes in life, it can be the same way, you may get so exhausted with all your responsibilities. You may be the kind of person who tries to fix everything and be everything for everyone, but remember, at some point you need a refill in your mental, spiritual, and physical containers. You must take the time to slow down long enough for a refill or you may find yourself desperately pushing, only to find the output is not enough because you are nearly empty. You may be so desperate to get the last few drops in a dispenser, you will shake the container, apply pressure, and keep pushing, but this does not help and can lead to a broken, damaged, and defective container.

The same is true in life. You must take time to replenish all that you have poured out. You may be pushing yourself so hard that you have nothing left and continuing to push can lead to brokenness and can be harmful to your mental and physical health.

Clogged and Cluttered

When a dispenser is not working properly, it is often because it is obstructed. It could be clogged from filling it with the wrong material, or the spring may be damaged or broken from pushing too quickly and too frequently.

The same is true in life. You may face obstacles, and the spring in your step may diminish or break from overuse or misuse. You must remember to make time to refill, replenish, and replace what you have given of yourself and poured into the lives of others. Remember, it is not selfish to take care of yourself first; in fact, it is crucial because you can only give what you have.

When you are constantly pouring out of yourself, giving your time, talents, love, patience, and energy, you must make time to replenish and refill, or eventually, you will have nothing left to give.

CLOSING

THIS BOOK IS dedicated to all my family and friends. I am extremely grateful to everyone who has inspired me, encouraged me, and pushed me to make this book a reality. It is my hope that the principles in this book will help you develop a positive new approach to seeing the extraordinary hidden amid the ordinary. We all have different dreams, goals, and beliefs, but I believe the principles outlined in this book can help you become someone who always sees the best, is grateful for the little things, and lives a productive, positive, and successful life.

Thank you for your purchase. I would love to hear from you. If you have questions, comments, or suggestions please email them to booksbydrdavinasmith@gmail.com